T0113888

RESET
IN GOD'S PRESENCE

MOVING FROM RELIGION TO RELATIONSHIP FOR
EMOTIONAL AND SPIRITUAL FITNESS

CHERYL POLKE

WESTBOW
PRESS®
A DIVISION OF THOMAS NELSON
& ZONDERVAN

WestBow Press books may be ordered through booksellers or by contacting:

WestBow Press
A Division of Thomas Nelson & Zondervan
1663 Liberty Drive
Bloomington, IN 47403
www.westbowpress.com
844-714-3454

Scripture taken from the King James Version of the Bible.

ISBN: 978-1-6642-7716-8 (sc)
ISBN: 978-1-6642-7715-1 (e)

Print information available on the last page.

WestBow Press rev. date: 11/08/2022

CONTENTS

Forward..vii

Introduction ix

Chapter 1   Satan's Game Plan 1

Chapter 2   Salvation - Saved From What?... 8

Chapter 3   Spiritual Warfare - Demons are Real..14

Chapter 4   Encountering God.. 24

Chapter 5   Origins of Depression, Anxiety, Anger 32

Chapter 6   Bloody Victory Over Strongholds 35

Chapter 7   God's Love Never Fails 40

Chapter 8   Heart Level Healing and Change 46

Chapter 9   Spiritual and Behavioral Actions Against Depression...................... 48

Chapter 10   Spiritual and Behavioral Actions Against Anxiety, Fear, and Panic Attacks 52

Chapter 11   Spiritual and Behavioral Actions Against Anger 57

Chapter 12   Ministry Steps to Freedom for Self and Others 61

Chapter 13   Abiding in Christ and the Armor of God.. 64

Chapter 14   Birthing or Aborting Prayers 69

Chapter 15   Daily Reset in God 72

Appendix A. Ministry Prayers 77

References 87

FORWARD

Having worked in the field of psychology for thirty-five years, I am well aware that there are many people, including Christians, who suffer with anxiety, panic, worry, anger, sadness and depression. Sometimes these maladies are genetic and are inherited biologically through the generations. Sometimes they are passed down in a family as learned behavior, and sometimes they are reactions to current life stressors. It is not unusual that people, good people, do not have the knowledge and coping skills that they need to overcome these troublesome emotions and the negative thoughts that fuel them. Christians are not exempt from life's misfortunes. I have often said, "Everyone has a story." If you have reached your mid-twenties, you have likely experienced some sort of hardship because life is often difficult and unpredictable. As a psychologist, I have also seen people heal and change their behaviors, their emotions, and their lives through our therapeutic work. In addition, one of the important tenets of Christianity is physical, emotional, and spiritual healing.

This book, Resent in God's Presence, can be thought of as a program of spiritual growth, guiding, the reader to encouragement and healing. We are created to know God and to be in a close and loving relationship with God. God wants us to be healthy and joy-filled, and He is able to reset us in that direction as we spend time in His Presence. The book is designed to help you to remove anything that would hinder your abiding intimacy with Christ. Some of what Cheryl Polke recommends in her book are solid psychological techniques, such as nutritional advice, and deep breathing, but most of what she offers is spiritual and Biblical.

There have been reliable surveys over the years, such as by the Pew Research Center, that indicate that praying people with positive religious beliefs are generally happier than those without. Reset in God's Presence is a practical help to anyone who seeks to improve his or her state of mind, behavior, and mood using beliefs and practices of Christianity. The plan that the book outlines is based not so much upon rules and principles, but upon a living, loving relationship with the Creator of the Universe, communicating with God and spending time in God's Presence. Maybe you did not think that was possible, but if you follow Ms. Polke's lead, you will be delighted to learn that it is.

There are many ways to seek healing including the laying on of hands, casting out spirits, anointing with oil, declaring healing, or declaring Scripture verses. Another, rarely taught method, is resting and abiding in God's Presence.

Ms. Polke is a Registered Nurse who has worked in a variety of settings, including state mental health hospitals and working with the severely disabled. She has seen the devastation of emotional and mental health suffering. She is a Christian who has been listening to the Lord for years. She has ministered to others of all ages, especially to young people, and has taught and trained people in this spiritual plan. This book is a down-to earth approach to spiritual, cognitive and emotional health and wellness. Ms. Polke and I have been friends for decades and we have known the difficulties in each other's lives. I have seen changes in her as she has used these techniques herself. I see that she is calmer, happier, kinder and more content, all desirable traits. I encourage you to sit yourself down with Reset in God's Presence, incorporate the practices that she outlines, and open your heart to endless possibilities of intimacy with God and your subsequent and inevitable healing.

Marguerite Mosack, Ph.D., Psychologist

INTRODUCTION

I practiced professional nursing on various levels and positions predominantly in the field of mental health for over 35 years. The field of psychiatry and psychology is excellent at identifying symptoms in order to formulate a diagnosis. I experienced the limitations of a system that excluded the manufacturer's manual on the use and repair of the human soul and spirit. God (Father, Son, Spirit) is the master designer who knows how to reset one emotionally, physically, and spiritually into His promised abundant life. We live in a world that has for the most part rejected the notion of a personal God who is more than willing to deliver those from their inner painful worlds if but they would believe in Him.

God sees emotional issues no differently than He sees physical infirmities. He is near the broken hearted and knows the trauma, abuse, rejection, abandonment, poverty, physical disabilities, comparisons whether perceived or real that many individuals have faced from parents as well as other individuals in their lifetimes and some even before birth. These issues have far reaching effects on how one views themselves, others, God and even life itself. Emotional pain can drive many maladaptive behaviors and life decisions which like a slimy residue effects everyone it touches. Depression, fear, and anger can create negative outcomes in every area of life including physical, financial, relational, spiritual, and of course emotional. This book will provide the reader with hope for real change in one's life. This change is founded on the love and power of God that is available to all who would come to him and learn His ways. This book is different in that it teaches relationship empowers and religion brings frustration. I have personally changed more in the last few years through moving from religion to relationship.

You and I were created to have a real dynamic loving relationship with God. This book will offer the reader a God driven plan to reset their inner world of negative thoughts and emotions based on the bible along with learning to abide in God's presence. This resetting will cast out fear and panic, overcome depression, restore healthy loving relationships, offer peace, and hope to anyone who will take the time to work through its pages and discover this beautiful Savior and Lord Jesus Christ who said, "I am come that they might have life, and that they might have it more abundantly." John 10:10.

Everyone will need to confront fear in this hour whether they are new to Christianity or are a seasoned believer in Him. This book will teach one how to enter into a daily position of trusting in the perfect character of God and the truthfulness of his Word while removing the lies and half-truths embedded in our souls which keep us from resting fully in Him. Reset in God's Presence has very practical step by step guidance and directions on walking into freedom from anxiety, depression and more as you learn to become an overcomer fighting the good fight of faith.

My prayer is that you will learn how to gain daily freedom from your negative emotions as you move into a personal, powerful abiding walk with the One who deserves our utmost worship in exchange for the abundant life. You will step into Him and all He has for you.

Special note: My dad whom I refer to in the book, became a great support to me as an adult. I was privileged to pray with him to accept Christ as his Savior and Lord one year before he died.

God bless

1
SATAN'S GAME PLAN

Let us consider the account of the fall of man in the book of Genesis. Anything a human being could ever want they had, right? They had a perfect relationship with God, the world, and each other. So, what went wrong?

Enter Satan, the Father of Lies. Satan began to inject the insidious thought to the first woman that God was withholding something from her. This something he whispered to her, could result in a greater level of fulfillment and autonomy. "Come on," Satan would say, "look at the beautiful luscious looking fruit on the tree of the knowledge of good and evil. There must be something special in fruit so desirable." She was intrigued and discussed the matter with Satan. The evil one slyly accused God of lying when he responded to the first woman with, "You shall not surely die, for God knows that in the day you eat of it your eyes will be opened and you will be like God, knowing the difference between good and evil," Genesis:2-17, King James Version. "It does not make sense as to why God would tell you that you would surely die from something that looks so good. Could it be that God does not want you to be a god yourself?"

NO EXPERIENTIAL KNOWLEDGE OF EVIL

The first man and woman had no experiential knowledge of evil but they did know right from wrong. Adam was given the command from God not to eat of the tree of the knowledge of good and evil. They both made a free will choice to reject the known goodness of God . Adam may have relinquished his authority to his wife allowing the willful rebellion to take place. The seduction to gain personal power and control through the knowledge of evil seduced Adam and Eve. It continues to seduce many to this present day.

Why did God allow this horrific wrong choice to take place? God said in Genesis, "Let us make man in our image," Genesis 1:26. The Triune God agreed that man would be made with a free will so he could choose to be in right relationship with Him. I believe inherent in this statement was also the knowledge of the fall of man and the plan of salvation through the Incarnate Word. Man was created sinless but only God is infinitely good. He is perfect in every aspect of His eternal being. Contemplating the immeasurable glory and magnitude of who God is compared to his created beings can give a glimpse into understanding the fall of man.

DECEPTION — CALLING GOOD EVIL AND EVIL GOOD

An opportunity to express free will had to be given to the first human beings. God created man and woman to choose to love Him without coercion and to believe in His word. Satan's plan is to deceive and to call good evil and evil good. Satan will always attempt to cast doubt on the goodness of God and the truthfulness of His Word. One way he does this is by showing us all the pain and suffering in the world, and even in our own lives.

An opportunity to express free-will had to be given to the first human beings.

But how can you trust someone's word if you do not believe that they are absolute goodness? I grew up in a somewhat violent, poor household with an emotionally distant father who had unpredictable, explosive, angry outbursts. When I came to Christ, I thought God was powerful (like I saw my dad to be) but not very relational, provisional, or kind. I did want to believe and trust the Lord and His Word. The bible verses that spoke of His goodness, kindness and provision were difficult for me to embrace with any kind of faith. The evil one knows we obtain our vision of who God is or is not primarily through our fathers.

God conveyed to me several times over the years that I needed to know that He is good. While fasting and praying in 1997, He impressed me with the following: if I do not believe that He is good, I would not believe that He would take care of me and I would be just as afraid as everyone else. This was an ominous warning of future event(s). He also highlighted the following verses: "That we may have boldness in the day of judgment," followed by "There is no fear in love, but perfect love casteth out fear," 1John 4:17-18. This verse speaks of having confidence in God's care and love for you, not fear during time(s) of His judgments or calamities and great difficulties in the earth. We can believe His ways and His acts are always good according to Romans 8:28: "All things work together for good for those who love the Lord."

ACCUSING GOD OF WRONGDOING

I was a person of prayer before making Christ my Lord and Savior and I prayed even more after I received Him. However, as faithfully as I had prayed, I became incredibly angry at God for not answering my prayers as I thought he would and within my timing. God impressed on me that I had reduced Him to being human and that His thoughts and ways are so much higher than mine.

Whenever we are disappointed or even angry at God, we are accusing Him of wrongdoing just as Eve had done. My disappointment in not getting what I asked for in prayer fueled a slow burning resentment toward Him. I had to repent of my accusations that God was in error and my subsequent feelings of anger toward God. I had to repent of my judgements which characterized God as being imperfect. When we reduce God to being human our expectations of Him are hindered. We limit God to a human's finite thoughts and ways. I was instantly delivered from my resentment toward Him the moment he allowed me to see my error. God is gracious and merciful. When we face the truth about our feelings, resentments, judgments, or opinions of others, and especially of God, we can begin to grow, to heal, and to live in true reality.

Whenever we are disappointed or angry at God, we are accusing Him of wrongdoing just as Eve had done.

FORGIVENESS

We cannot forgive God because He is perfect but we are commanded to forgive others. Forgiveness is not a feeling. Forgiveness does not require warm feelings toward the one who offended us. Rather it is a spiritual decision which means you have chosen to agree with God that it is His will for you to forgive. Although it can be difficult to forgive, his grace is sufficient to enable you to do so. When you choose to forgive, you are giving up your right to hold anger, bitterness and even hatred toward the individual, organization, or a body of people for their action or inaction. You are forsaking revenge and letting God determine the judgement.

It is important to forgive all who have contributed to our hurts and bondages. We must also forgive someone that has something against us as well as take steps to reconcile according to God's Word. "Therefore if thou bring thy gift to the altar, and there rememberest that thy brother hath ought against thee; leave there thy gift before the altar and go thy way; first be reconciled to thy brother," Matthew 5:23-24.

God's Word also says He will not forgive us if we do not forgive those who harm us. We often think of forgiveness as doing a favor for the person who offended us, but forgiveness will set you free from the negative spiritual, emotional, and physical effects of the sin of unforgiveness. Choosing unforgiveness opens us up to demonic torments of anger, bitterness, negative ruminations, anxiety, insomnia and other physical illnesses and conditions and emotional isolation.

Human beings are capable of causing unspeakable damage to others. A severely wounded person may need time to work through painful memories or suppressed memories before reaching a place of forgiveness. A person's damaged emotions may need time to harmonize with their initial choice to forgive. Our God is near the broken hearted and His Spirit of Power and Truth, the Holy Spirit enables one to forgive.

For your own benefit learn to practice a daily lifestyle of pre-emptive or instant forgiveness. It is easier to prevent a problem than it is to fix one. God's word says, offences will come. God taught me to be prepared for offences before they happen. Your enemy likes to catch you off guard so that you will respond in an ungodly manner. It is helpful to know what can still offend and choose at the beginning of each day to walk in forgiveness regarding these triggers or other negative comments or actions incurred by others. We do not have to respond to offense ourselves, as God will address the wrongful actions of another in His own way and time.

This does not mean you should not take corrective action toward someone who is committing illegal acts or abuse. Forgiveness is not:

1. enabling someone to continue or diminish their sin
2. response to an apology
3. deny or cover up what happened
4. instant trust or even immediate reconciliation.

SPIRIT OF OFFENSE

A spirit of offense is feeling resentful because of an actual or perceived insult. Adam and Eve had become offended at God. They harbored the idea that God was withholding something good from them. The enemy implied God was keeping them from becoming gods themselves. A spirit of offense is truly a doorway for the enemies' follow-up punch of deception. I became victim to this 1-2 punch when I had become offended by many individual Christians. I subsequently labeled the Church collectively as the problem. Thankfully, I heard a powerful message on being offended that convicted me of this sin. Offense followed by Satan's tool of deception can even lead to heresy which is profoundly serious. John the Baptist is an example of this offense/deception doorway. He identified Jesus as the lamb of God who takes away the sins of the world, then upon his imprisonment he requested his disciples to ask Jesus if He was the Messiah. Did the enemy cause John to change his mind about Jesus' true identity after he went to prison. Jesus responded and cautioned his listeners with "blessed is he who is not offended at me." How easy it is for us to become offended at God and others. We need to acknowledge when we have been offended by God and others and to quickly shut the door on the spirits of offense and deception by repenting and forgiving as God commands. Depending on the seriousness of the offense a discussion with the person(s) involved may be indicated as well.

No one has had perfect parents except Adam and Eve. So, it is understandable how we view God through the lens of imperfection.

Our views about God many times can be traced back to our opinion of our parents whether good, bad, or in-between. No one has had perfect parents except Adam and Eve. So having seen imperfection in our own parents, it is understandable how we view God through the lens of imperfection. The first book of James notes that a double minded man will receive nothing that he asks for. A double minded man is one who does not believe that God is always good. He believes Him some of the time then not at other times depending on what he is experiencing. Our human finite concept of goodness cannot define Who God is. His eternal character expressed in His Word the Bible does. .

It is important for us to see the heinousness that man's rebellion(sin) against God birthed into us. Man's choice to turn away from God's authority has infected all humanity and continues to impact us all to this day. "For the flesh lusts against the Spirit, and the Spirit against the flesh, and these are contrary to one another, so that you do not do the things that you wish," Galatians 5:17.

SATAN'S LEGAL RIGHTS

Satan gained legal access to humans through their decision to choose evil over good . He seduced mankind into believing that the God of the bible and His Son cannot be trusted or believed in. He instructs the world through false religions, philosophies, psychology, etc. through which people can follow gods of their own creation including self as seen in the religion of humanism. Satan, who envisions himself a god, encourages us to reject the one true God of the Bible and His plan to restore humanity to its true destiny and purpose found only in Christ.

GOD'S WORD AND BIBLICAL LAWS

God's word is not a legal battering ram used to bring condemnation on mankind. John 3:17 says, "For God sent not His Son into the world to condemn the world, but that the world through Him might be saved." God's word instead shows us righteousness vs. unrighteousness or what sin is and how it affects our relationship to God. Unrepented sin allows the enemy access to our lives bringing destruction. Satan always tries to move us into the realm of unbelief whether it be in the form of a deceptive mixture of truth and lies or strong feelings that deny the truth of God's character and His Word because we are unable to see evidence of God's goodness in our natural circumstances. Repentance for ignorance or unbelief of God's word will bring life giving healing and wholeness as God intends for His people.

God's biblical laws which relate to judgements held against others but especially our parents remain in effect even if we do not know the laws or do not believe the laws are for today. Deuteronomy 26:16, "Cursed is anyone who dishonors his father or his mother." Matt: 7:1-2 says, "Judge not, that ye be not judged. For with what judgment ye judge, ye shall be judged and with what measure ye meted, it shall be measured to you again." Hebrews 12:15 says, " Looking diligently lest any man fail of the grace of God; lest any root of bitterness springing up trouble you, and thereby many be defiled."

In any area(s) where one dishonors a parent repeatedly through sin or judging them (even if the judgement is true) one may reap that dishonor or judgment in his or her life. These judgements are usually formulated during childhood or adolescence and involves branding those judged with an unredeemable sin or character flaw. This judgement reflects one's poor estimation of God's ability to change the parent. An example of judging one's parents can be the following: you may have judged your dad for his out-of-control raging; therefore you may reap that judgment in your life by possibly marrying someone with an anger problem or you may develop a raging problem yourself. An example of a bitterroot judgement would be expecting or believing all men to act a certain way based on your judgement of your father.

Identifying and repenting of those areas of dishonor or judgements through the power of the Holy Spirit removes Satan's legal right to reciprocate or bring that judgement into your life and also brings God's plan of restoration and redemption to you.

It is difficult to believe God's word if one does not believe in the perfect character of God. "But without faith it is impossible to please Him; for he that cometh to God must believe that He is and that He is a rewarder of them that diligently seek Him," Hebrews 11:6. Knowing God daily as absolute goodness is a foundational key to being able to enter a consistent, trusting, and abiding relationship with Him. The brutal death, burial, and resurrection of Jesus Christ for sinners is the greatest demonstration of God's love and goodness for all eternity. His forgiveness of undeserving repentant sinners is magnificent!

I hope I have stressed how important it is to hold a high opinion of God's character and His word. This will enable you to trust Him, no matter what you experience in life. The evil one will use every opportunity to create a wedge between you and God through challenging times. He employs our emotions, thoughts, friends, etc. to produce doubt and discontent while we navigate rough waters. "Be sober, be vigilant; because your adversary the devil, as a roaring lion, walketh about, seeking whom he may devour,"1 Peter 5:8. I write this so that you can be warned and prepared for the good fight of faith.

Praying with a pastor, minister or counselor considering the following points may be helpful if you have difficulty in believing that God is good:

- You may have projected onto God the negative characteristics of your parent(s) especially your father/mother or other authority figure(s) during your childhood.
- Forgive the authority person(s) in your life for any sin committed against yourself or for not meeting a need of yours while growing up. Note: it is helpful to make a list for each parent or authority person that raised you or had a strong effect on you as a child or teen identifying those sins committed against you and the judgments you made toward them (see next point).
- Create a list of what you didn't like about each parent (dead or alive) and what you wished they would have done for you as a child/teen (dead or alive).
- Ask God to forgive you for judging your parents for their negative characteristics, things they did or didn't do for you based on God's word in Matt: 7:2, which says," for what judgment ye judge ye shall be judged."

- Repent of any anger toward God for unanswered prayers.
- Keep a list of times God has shown Himself good in your life and review it often.
- Do a study on the brutal torture and murder of Jesus Christ for you a sinner.
- Allow God Himself to reveal His goodness to you through His Word and His Presence.

Repentance Prayers for Dishonoring Our Parents, Our Judgements of them, and Our Bitter Root Expectations:

Fill in the blanks with your dishonoring sin(s) toward your parents, judgments of them and your possible subsequent bitter root expectations. (Note: pray these prayers for each individual area identified):
1. Dear Lord forgive me for dishonoring my mother/father for _____: chronic disobedience, refusing to listen to them, being stubborn and rebellious, lying to them, verbal or physical aggression, disrespect, lack of affection, hatred, stealing from them, mocking or walking away from them when they are talking, rolling your eyes or making huffing/puffing noises at them, lack of honoring them through birthdays, holidays, care or help they need, being grateful to them, etc.).
2. Dear Lord I forgive my _____ (mother/father) for treating me _____ (identify the hurtful words, actions) or not meeting my need for _____ (identify areas of lack such i.e., food, clothing, clean environment, affection both verbal and appropriate physical, attention, praise, help, etc.).
3. Lord forgive me for judging my _____ (mother/father) for being_____ (negative characteristic, habit, lifestyle etc. that you disliked about them).
4. Lord forgive me for the bitter root expectation of _____ (identify the expectation based on judging your parents e.g., that all women or all men will act or eventually treat you in like manner).
5. Lord, I thank you for forgiving me as I place all these sins on the cross based on your word in 1 John 1:9 which says if we confess our sins, he is faithful and just to forgive us our sins and to cleanse us from all unrighteousness.

2
SALVATION - SAVED FROM WHAT?

An opportunity to express free will had to be given to the first human beings. God created man and woman to choose to love Him without coercion and to believe in His word and character as stated earlier. Everything God does has significant meaning and giving the first man only one law to adhere to was very meaningful. The number one represents unity in scripture. The first man/woman chose to make Satan's words first in their life which broke the unity or intimacy they had with God. Their choice was a direct rejection of God Himself and forfeited the glory of God's eternal life that was given to them. God warned them that if they ate of the tree of the knowledge of good and evil that surely, they would die. Scripture does not give information regarding

Adam and Eve's grievous choice to believe Satan over God opened the portal for knowing death. They went from being immortal to being mortal.

their comprehension of physical and or spiritual death. There was no experiential or observational knowledge of death in the garden. Their grievous choice to believe Satan over God opened the portal for knowing death. They went from being immortal to being mortal.

The first man and woman started out in perfect relationship with God and then lost it. Because of their choice all humans inherit spiritual death. This spiritual death means one has no relationship with God. Many people are DECEIVED into thinking they have a relationship with God because they pray prayers that are seemingly answered, they attend church, or they believe that they are good people.

GOD'S PLAN TO RESTORE MAN TO HIMSELF

The Good NEWS or the Gospel is that Jesus Christ came to restore relationship for us back to God the Father through His death, burial, and resurrection. "For God so loved the world that He gave His only begotten son that whosoever believeth in Him should not perish, but have everlasting life," John 3:16. Because of sin, humans have great difficulty comprehending the absolute purity and perfection of a Holy God. Spiritual death and separation from God entered through one man's disobedient life. Life would be restored through One man's obedience unto death. God's word says life is in the blood. This is the reason a perfect human blood sacrifice was required penalty or payment for sin. Christ alone accomplished what no other human could do. Christ's blood was never tainted with sin. He always did Father God's will. He alone lived a perfect life. All humans have sinned at least once and have not kept God's laws perfectly. "All have sinned and come short of the glory of God," Romans 3:23. Jesus Christ was fully God but became fully human to undo what was done by the first man and woman.

CHANGED FROM DARKNESS TO LIGHT - MY STORY

God draws a person to Jesus through His Holy Spirit. "No man can come to Me, except the Father which hath sent Me draw Him," John 6:44. God is so good that He initiates this incredible relationship with Himself. Here is my story: I grew up in a denomination that did not stress the need for salvation but stressed the need for good works. I had feelings of love for Jesus as a child and adolescent. Assurance that God was real and that He was answering my prayers for help had evaded me. My family and I went to services weekly and I tried to do what I thought was right. I often felt anxious, depressed, and insecure depending upon my circumstances and the behaviors of others towards me. By the time I reached my late twenties I was a very unhappy individual.

But God was drawing me. I began to read the bible and would abruptly close it when I discovered I was doing what the bible commanded not to do. I started to read other spiritual books too that promoted self more than God. I knew Jesus was who I was looking for and if the book did not mention Jesus, I knew it was not true. That revelation alone had to be from God.

My unhappiness was the fuel to search out if God really existed. In hindsight I was really looking more for happiness than God at that time but God in His goodness kept the light on for me. A professor in one of my college classes said, "If you really want to be happy give your life to Jesus." I had just learned the key to happiness so I was eager to find out how to do this. No one that I knew could tell me. Christian television became a significant avenue God used to draw me. One day I heard a man on the 700 Club say, "Pray this prayer with me if you want to give your life to Jesus."

Here was my long-awaited answer, so I prayed with him. My heart by this point in time was willing to do whatever God wanted. Instantly I was aware that I was a sinner and the manner I had been living was wrong. This sense of being a sinner lifted and then I knew that I knew that God was real. I prayed, "God I want everything you have for me." I was what the bible calls born again and had now come out of the kingdom of darkness and into His kingdom of light, John 3:3, "except a man be born again, he cannot see the kingdom of God." I was overwhelmed with joy in knowing that God was real and could now sense a relationship with Him. My conversion to Christ connected me to God through the new indwelling of the Holy Spirit. I was instantly changed and had new desires in my heart to follow God and do what was pleasing to Him. The bible became desirable and understandable. I can still remember that glorious day. I no longer rejected God's gift of salvation found in the person of Jesus Christ and therefore was not considered a sinner by God's standards as stated, "And such were some of you; but ye are washed, but ye are sanctified, but ye are justified in the name of the Lord Jesus and by the Spirit of our God," I Corinthians 6:11.

The Lord baptized or filled me with his Holy Spirit when I asked him to give me everything He had for me as in Acts 4:31, "and they were all filled with the Holy Ghost, and they spoke the word of God with boldness." This infilling of the Holy Spirit is not the same as what takes place at conversion. It is a subsequent empowerment to be a bold witness in all areas of our life and ministry for Christ. Pray and ask God initially to baptize you with His Holy Spirit and then to fill you daily.

SAVED FOR A LIFE WITH HIM AND FROM AN ETERNAL LIFE WITHOUT HIM

God's word says, "that if thou shalt confess with your mouth the Lord Jesus, and shalt believe in thine heart that God hath raised him from the dead, thou shalt be saved." Saved for and from what though? God does not force anyone to choose Him. To choose Him means to choose His life now and for eternity. Life in Christ now is to be saved from living life in your strength without His indwelling Spirit and power to overcome sin, i.e. unbelief in God the Father, Son and Holy Spirit, anxiety, depression, selfishness, greed, unrighteous anger, etc. God's word says, "whatsoever is not of faith is sin," Romans 14:23. Faith is belief in God and His Word.

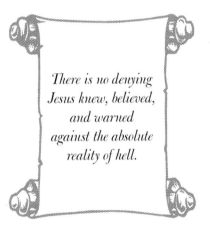

There is no denying Jesus knew, believed, and warned against the absolute reality of hell.

To not choose God during your lifetime means you willingly have rejected God's gift of salvation and chosen spiritual death now and for eternity. You will enter eternity at the time of your physical death without any relationship to God. This death is an eternal separation from God who is the originator and giver of all that is good. If all good things such as air, breathing, comfort, hope, light, love, relationships, rest, water, etc. are from God, what would an existence be like without them? It sounds like hell, doesn't it? There is no denying Jesus knew, believed, and warned against the absolute reality of hell.

Make no doubt you ultimately choose God or reject God before entering eternity upon your death. God's will be that no man should perish.

What does it mean to confess with your mouth the Lord Jesus and believe that God raised him from the dead? Confession is a choice to agree or to admit something is true. Confession is also done aloud with one's mouth. Believing that salvation is only available through Jesus Christ is made possible through God's grace or empowerment. He enables one to believe but make no mistake you ultimately choose God or reject God. God's will be that no man should perish or go to hell. Believing in the Lordship of Jesus Christ is to submit to His Spirit and His Word (the Bible) .

Merely making a public confession of these truths at some point is not proof that you are genuinely saved. In 2 Corinthians 13:5, God's word says, "Examine yourselves, whether you are in the faith."

Do you now have a relationship with God based on John 14:15, "If you love me, keep my commandments." Are you now living in righteousness or right living according to God's word by the power of the Holy Spirit. Living in righteousness characterizes true conversion. There will be a change in your heart and lifestyle when you transfer from the kingdom of darkness into the kingdom of light. The Bible makes it clear that only those who recognize their sinfulness and need for a Savior can enter the Kingdom of God. A willingness to turn from the world's ways of living to God's ways is required. This turning is called repentance and this spiritual change will be evident to self and to others.

HE CAME TO SEEK AND SAVE THE LOST

Prior to my coming to Christ I knew of Him in name but did not know for sure if He was even real. The day I prayed to invite Christ into my heart in 1985 was the day that I knew that I knew that I knew He was REAL. A favorite activity of mine since then has been telling others that God exists and sharing the gospel with them. It is even more exciting when He shows them, He exists by manifesting His presence or displaying the gifts of the Holy Spirit.

Here are just a few stories to show you the love God has for those who do not know Him yet. I look back on these events with great awe of how powerful and merciful God is and how He loves to use us.

While in Spain on a short-term mission trip, my interpreter and I met several young adults on the street. We attempted to share Jesus with them. They were smirking and nudging each other, basically mocking us. I asked the one young guy if he knew that he looked like Tom Cruise. He nodded and said yes. This got his attention and we then asked if we could pray for him and his friends. They looked at each other and then gave a reluctant nod. I began to pray for the Lord to bless the Tom Cruise look alike with the money that he needed. He and his friends literally began to cry. I did not know that the young man had a drug dealer harassing him for money he owed. It was not just the words that were prayed but the presence of the Holy Spirit that moved them to tears and allowed us to share the gospel of Jesus Christ with them. During this same trip we shared the gospel with a group of about twenty young girls. They joined hands together and the presence of the Holy Spirit was so tangible that myself and my interpreter began to cry. All twenty young girls prayed to come to Christ. Alleluia!!!

We were walking down the street on our day off from sharing Jesus on this same trip. In Spain it is impolite to say hello to strangers, but an older woman and her daughter (we discovered) said hello to us. I said to my interpreter, Loli, say hello back to them, obviously God is doing something here.

The woman and her daughter then invited us to come back with them to their apartment. We talked with them for 2 hours about Jesus and needing to be born again, etc. They both prayed to come to Christ, and we heard they were both baptized and faithfully attending one of the churches we were working with in Spain. Glory to God.

One evening God impressed on me to go down to the bar section of our town where young adults socialize. A friend came with me. I was handing out bible tracks to anyone who would take one. There were two young guys who allowed us to share a bit. They both began to argue with us. I said, we do not want to argue with you, but can we pray for you? They agreed, bowed their heads, and held our hands and I prayed, Lord give Jim a job and Joe a girlfriend. The one young man grabbed my arm and said how did you know that? I said know what? He said, I need a job and Joe is looking for a girlfriend. My friend and I were speechless. He then said to our surprise we want what you have because what you have is for real. They both prayed to come to Christ. Faithful God.

Another time God impressed on me to go to a specific restaurant alone. Cannot say that I did not struggle with that one a bit, but I went. A waitress came over to me and started telling me about her abusive boyfriend. I said would you like to sit down, pointing to the empty seat across from me. She said no but sat down anyway. We talked for a bit and then I shared Jesus with her. I said would you like to invite Jesus into your heart? She said, no. The thought came to me to bind that demon up. I bowed my head briefly and prayed to bind the demon keeping her from coming to Christ. I looked up and said, How about now? She said yes and prayed to come to Christ. What a powerful Savior we have.

During a time of fasting and praying the thought came to me I needed a revelation of hell. I went into the Christian bookstore and to my amazement one of the best seller books was called a Divine Revelation of Hell. I purchased the book and read it. It literally scared the HELL out of me. I remember asking God am I really saved? Well I accidentally left the book on my mother's desk and my sister picked it up and read it. She used to bait me into arguments about being born again etc. and I was running out of patience with her (I was younger in the Lord then, SMILE!) . She called me and asked what she had to do to be saved. I remember telling her this is the last time I am going to tell you, so I told her what she needed to do. She called me 3 days later and said she prayed the prayer and was now born again wanting to read the Bible. My sister is faithfully serving the Lord along with her husband. Isn't God Wonderful!

It is God's will that all people should be in relationship with Him. God draws men to Himself but He allows each person to willfully believe and follow Him. One is born again or birthed into the Kingdom of God through the Holy Spirit the moment one believes in Jesus as Savior and as Lord. A powerful supernatural transaction takes place during this rebirthing which is manifested in a change of heart and behavior. God also gives humans the choice to reject Him in this life which opens the door for an eternal life without Him.

PRAYER TO RECEIVE THE LORD JESUS CHRIST AS SAVIOR AND LORD:

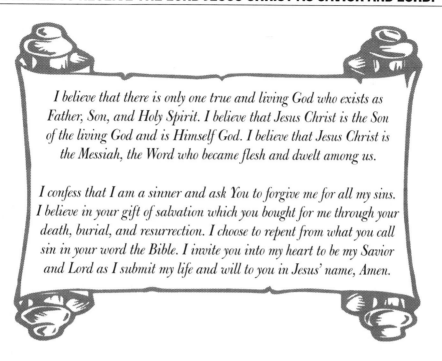

I believe that there is only one true and living God who exists as Father, Son, and Holy Spirit. I believe that Jesus Christ is the Son of the living God and is Himself God. I believe that Jesus Christ is the Messiah, the Word who became flesh and dwelt among us.

I confess that I am a sinner and ask You to forgive me for all my sins. I believe in your gift of salvation which you bought for me through your death, burial, and resurrection. I choose to repent from what you call sin in your word the Bible. I invite you into my heart to be my Savior and Lord as I submit my life and will to you in Jesus' name, Amen.

OUT OF THE KINGDOM OF DARKNESS AND INTO THE KINGDOM OF LIGHT

You are now a child of God as stated in John 5:24, "Verily, verily, I say unto you, He that heareth my word, and believeth on Him that sent me, hath everlasting life, and shall not come into condemnation, but is passed from death unto life."

Your sins in the past, present, and future have been forgiven and you have been justified by your faith in Jesus Christ. God commands us to confess our sins as we sin in 1 John 1:9, "If we confess our sins, He is faithful and just to forgive us our sins, and to cleanse us from all unrighteousness." Whenever you fall short of God's word, go to God, and confess your sin and receive His gracious forgiveness daily. He knows we are weak and as you depend on Him you will grow.

God's goal for you is that you be transformed into the image of His dear Son Jesus Christ. This is a daily process in which you cooperate and depend on the Holy Spirit by submitting your life and will to God. This is called sanctification. Remember, being a Christian is a daily relationship between you and your Lord which produces obedience based on love and gratefulness. You are no longer a sinner as you once were. Welcome into the Family of God. You are loved and chosen by the most wonderful being in the universe. Enjoy your Savior and Lord.

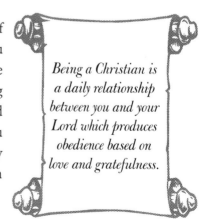

Being a Christian is a daily relationship between you and your Lord which produces obedience based on love and gratefulness.

3
SPIRITUAL WARFARE - DEMONS ARE REAL

Prior to receiving Jesus Christ as my Lord and Savior, I had opened doors for demonic oppression or access to my life through participating in and studying occult practices i.e., palm reading, fortune-telling, Ouija board, astrology, ESP, New Age healing and teaching, etc. I was looking for hope and direction for my life like many others who look to these occult practices.

God's word says in Deuteronomy 18:10: "There shall not be found among you anyone that maketh his son or his daughter to pass through the fire, or that useth divination, or an observer of times, or an enchanter, or a witch."

Divination according to the Merriam-Webster dictionary is :

> the art or practice that seeks to foresee or foretell future events or discover hidden knowledge usually by the interpretation of omens or by the aid of supernatural powers. Observer of times also indicates foreseeing the future. An enchanter or witch is one who casts spells, or curses on another. Both encompass the use of the magic arts.

TWO SOURCES OF POWER IN THE UNIVERSE

So why is that so bad and why does God forbid us from looking for help from these activities? Only two sources of power exist in the universe: the power that originates from God or power that God allows Satan to use. These activities as previously mentioned are not from God but from the evil one. Turning to Satan's arsenal of tools to help with our lives always comes with a jagged hook attached.

Turning to Satan's arsenal of tools to help with our lives always comes with a jagged hook attached.

The evil one hates you and me and his purpose is to kill, steal and destroy, John 10:10. Dabbling in these activities or using them to gain knowledge or control is dangerous. In essence you have turned to demons for help. God will not endure the placement of Satan on the throne of your life. This is called idolatry. God so abhors idolatry that He compares it to committing sexual immorality, Colossians.3:5. Can you see that the evil one always attempts to usurp the power and authority of God through mimicking the true power and gifts of God? Many Christians will discard the true things of God for fear of falling into the false. Fear is the lack of knowledge of perfect love only found in God's Word and intimacy with His Holy Spirit.

WAITING ON GOD

God wants us to trust and receive answers for our future, our healing, and our freedom through Him. He is a Good Father. God's will for us is to live and move and have our very being in Him through His Spirit and His Word, Acts 17:28. He wants us to grow in the fruit of the Spirit, which is "love, joy, peace, patience, kindness, goodness, faithfulness, gentleness, and self-control," Galatians 5:22.

Did you catch the word "patience?" Human beings want blessings and answers for our lives now. Our flesh does not like to seek and wait for God to answer or to bless us. We go running ahead and make things happen or turn to forbidden activities. This usually results in Satan's hooks, difficulties, or heartbreak which God never intended for us to have in our lives. Many blame God at times for the results of their poor sinful choices.

Satan tempted the Son of God by offering Him instant power and wealth if Jesus would bow and worship him. Submitting our lives to the evil one when we gratify the flesh through his ways, i.e., marijuana, alcohol, sex outside of marriage, etc. can be the same as bowing and worshipping Satan.

There is much fruit developed in the waiting on God.

There is much fruit developed in the waiting on God. During the waiting seasons of our lives, we are growing to know the Lord. Our character matures into a son or daughter of God that can be trusted to administer His love and power. "But let patience have its perfect work, that you may be perfect and complete, lacking nothing, James, 1:4. You are learning to become dependent on God's grace to overcome your weaknesses in order to fulfill the call or purpose for your life.

DECEPTIONS WHILE WAITING AND BATTLING UNBELIEF

God's work is to grow your faith. Satan's plan is to steal and to destroy your faith a little each day or all at once such as during a traumatic event. This is why it is important to have daily fellowship with the Lord who is the author and finisher of your faith, Hebrews 12:2. Faith is believing the truth of God's word and in His perfect character .

Your emotions and circumstances may speak one thousand times louder than God's Word or Spirit at times. The enemy is lying to you by saying God is not helping or even hearing you. Do not believe him. There may be many reasons for the wait or delay or seemingly unanswered prayer but it is not the reason the enemy has given you. God is for you and not against you. "For whatsoever is born of God overcometh the world: and this is the victory that overcometh the world, even our faith," I John 5:4.

Experiencing difficulty in believing God's Word offers us an opportunity to overcome the reason for our unbelief. Some of the reasons for unbelief may be due to the following:

1. Sin of unbelief that runs in your family line.
2. Wounded spirit/heart that believes a lie about God, self, others, life etc. that needs to be healed so it can receive the truth.
3. Vows (usually include "I will never" or "I will always," embedded in them) made in response to painful events or people .
4. Oaths made which usually contain "I am" statements in them.
5. Distortion of God's character based on projecting one's parents' flaws onto God.
6. Agreements one has made with other's negative opinions or curses made by others or even oneself, enemies' lies, cultural, educational, or religious untruths.
7. Judgments made toward others or sowing and reaping due to sinful behaviors.
8. Bitterroot expectations made in response to repetitive hurts by parents, family members, others, or circumstances.
9. Negative attitudes learned or developed in life.
10. Last but definitely not least, lack of time spent fellowshipping with God and studying His Word.

There may be a myriad of other reasons, but saying yes, to the process of growing in faith through patience will produce Christ's character in you. Jesus himself is your reward as you diligently seek Him and His righteousness. This focus orders things in the believer's life according to God's will.

Enoch was raptured by God because of His faith. The book of Hebrews says that he pleased God and without faith it is impossible to please God. Enoch walked with God as stated in the book of Genesis 5:24. The Hebrew meaning of the word walked implies that Enoch went up and down, in and out, back and forth, arm in arm with God, continually talking with Him and growing closer to Him. Enoch became less attached to the things of this world as he walked with God. His walk with God produced in him the kind of faith that pleases God. This kind of faith is born out of one who longs to know and to be with the one he loves. It is born out of intimacy which produced a man in the Faith Hall of Fame.

There were men and women of faith in the book of Hebrews who never received the promises but died in faith. How were they able to keep believing yet they never received? Jesus is the author and finisher of our faith. His Spirit will enable you to keep believing. When you feel your faith withering look to the Spirit of Truth and Power. He will give you all that you need to keep believing. Never quit believing in God and His Word.

GOING FROM GLORY TO GLORY

I want to be authentic with you in telling my journey with the Lord. Even though God miraculously delivered me from depression in 1994 I could still get very discouraged with my own growth and painful experiences in life. I said to the Lord, "I do not want you to pick me up out of the pit again only to know life will knock me back down." God in His still small voice said, "Cheryl, every time I pick you up, you are changed. You are going from glory to glory!" Not only was He the lifter of my head but He was the one who was taking me from strength to greater strength during these times of waiting for God's changes or blessings. When he spoke that to my spirit, I was instantly delivered from a sinful whining mindset. Now, that is power.

ENSLAVEMENT CHOICE BY CHOICE

The enemy also knows our weaknesses and wants to produce enslavement through our sinful choices, i.e., sexual immorality, alcohol, drugs, occult practices, etc. Remember, Satan is pure evil and his demons do not care if you understand that these doors give him legal right to your life. He does not care if you are three years old or hundred years old. Satan and his servants are legalists. This means whenever you chose his ways over God's ways this can open a door or a legal right for him in your life. He does not usually do it all at once nor do we sin greatly all at once. It is each individual choice made that can lead us into bondage. True freedom is found only in Christ and walking in daily submission to Him. He always leads us into victory, not death, defeat, anxiety, depression, etc.

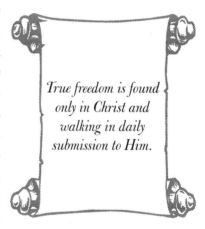

True freedom is found only in Christ and walking in daily submission to Him.

DEMONIZED HOUSE

I was a new Christian and little did I know, I had purchased a house that was demonized or haunted. I had all kinds of nightmares and saw apparitions appearing which looked like three dimensional crystals going through my walls at angles. I heard voices or sounds of furniture crashing that woke me up. Most of the activity occurred around 3 am. The third floor of this house always had flies in it. My sister and I together watched a basket fall at an angle off the refrigerator seven to eight feet onto the middle of the kitchen floor without any obvious cause.

I had an inner knowing that God was going to use this supernatural activity to teach me how to deal with the demonic realm. Sure enough, I made a friend at work who knew exactly what to do to stop the enemy from operating in my home. She brought a team of people over and we prayed through the house forbidding the enemy from manifesting and inhabiting my house in the mighty name of Jesus. They also anointed my doors and windows with blessed oil, symbolic of the Holy Spirit. Soon after this a friend at church gave me a recording of a Satanist now turned Christian. He said on the recording, "and some of you are having nightmares," and then prayed a prayer for the enemy to go. I agreed with his prayer. All tormenting activity including the nightmares stopped. Glory to God.

AUTHORITY OVER DEMONIC FORCES

Jesus through the finished work of the cross has given the Church all authority over the works of the enemy. Agreeing with the enemy either knowingly or unknowingly gives Satan's troops legal right to harass and oppress. Any area of God's word that we are not in agreement with through disobedience or ignorance gives the enemy an opportunity to attack and possibly enslave. God says,"My people are destroyed for lack of knowledge," Hosea 4:6. Does the enemy oppress everyone the same? No, not really. He can estimate the call and purpose on one's life better than most of us can. His intelligence and cunning surpass that of humans. He is and remains a created being though and does not compare to the omniscient, omnipotent, omnipresent, eternal Triune God.

Demonic forces do tempt us to sin and disobey God. Should we allow demons to succeed in these attacks or temptation, demonic oppression results. Continued sin or disobedience to God's word increases the demons influence over one's thoughts, behavior, and spirituality. God tells us in His Word that we are to "Submit yourselves therefore to God and resist the devil and he will flee from you." James 4:7.

When we choose to sin and yes, some sins are <u>more grievous</u> to God than others, we break fellowship with Him. We choose to walk out of the light and into the darkness. He does not leave us or stop loving us when we sin but will convict us of our sin in an effort to draw us back to Himself. God's word says, "I will never leave you nor forsake thee." Hebrews 13:5. According to His word, He helps us to want to do the right thing and then gives us the power to accomplish it, Phil: 2:13; "For it is God which worketh in you both to will and to do of his good pleasure."

But understand, we never lose our free will to choose God's way which leads to life or to choose sin which ultimately leads to death. God forgives when we repent but sin can have far reaching consequences lasting a lifetime and even infect ones' lineage.

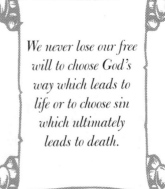

We never lose our free will to choose God's way which leads to life or to choose sin which ultimately leads to death.

The following is a list of occult activities and sins that open doors for demonic oppression:

- Occult practices - astral projection, astrology, bloody Mary (slumber party game), black/white magic, casting hexes or spells, channeling, crystal ball or spherical gemstones, clairvoyance, conjuration, divination, dungeons and dragons, ESP, fortune telling, horoscopes, hypnosis, levitation, martial arts, mediumship, mental telepathy, necromancy, Ouija board, palm reading, pendulum reading, praying to dead people, Satan worship, seances, spirit guides, tarot cards, tattoos, voodoo, werewolves and vampires, Wicca, witchcraft, yoga.
- Idolatry of the heart - anything that you prioritize over God, such as family, money, security, prestige, people, etc.
- False religions - Any religion that does not proclaim that Jesus Christ is God who came in the flesh and that there is only one way to God through Jesus Christ's death, burial, and resurrection for the forgiveness of sins
- Addictions - pornography, alcohol, recreational drugs or substances, gambling, sex, food, shopping etc.
- Abortion/Murder/Attempted Suicide
- Anger/Hatred
- Deception - lying, slander, fraud, cheating, infidelity, false representations, concealing the truth
- Trauma/Violence
- Sexual Immorality: any sex outside of marriage as defined in the Bible
- Unforgiveness

INANIMATE OBJECTS (DEMONIC PORTALS/ATTRACTIONS)

The demonic realm is real, and demons are looking for a body or an object in which to attach. Spirits can attach to objects that are not of the Lord, have been cursed, or dedicated to a false god. God calls objects that have been used in idolatry, occult activities, and the like as cursed items. Satan loves nothing more than for us to unknowingly open a door for him through what we wear, listen to, decorate our homes, cars, offices, and yards with. I strongly recommend you pray and ask the Holy Spirit to lead you to objects etc. that need to be discarded or destroyed. "Neither shalt though bring an abomination into thine house lest you be a cursed thing like it," Deuteronomy 7:26.

Generalized list of Items to discard or destroy as the Holy Spirit and His Word lead you:

- Videos/Movies/Games/Books/Pictures/Music with the following content: occult/new age/ witchcraft//immorality/violence/perversion/murder.
- Statues/Artwork/Jewelry/Clothing with/without symbols:
  Satanic, false/ancient gods, saints, false religions or philosophies, occult, witchcraft, crosses that are broken, inverted, or altered.
- Amulets (good luck charms):

This can range from something as simple as a lucky penny to using the colors of doors to promote good luck.
- Things used for spiritism:
dream catchers, crystals, Ouija boards

Just recently I purchased a necklace that had the symbols of yin/yang on it. This symbol originates in ancient Chinese mythology. The yin represents earth, passive, female, weak or dark and the yang symbol signifies heaven, active, positive, male, strong or light. I had a foul dream the night I wore it not recognizing the symbols. Once I found out the meaning and origin of the symbol, I threw the necklace away. The foul dreams stopped.

REPENTANCE GOD'S PATTERN/PROMISE

It is important to find out the reason that you or the person being ministered to has opened these doors and then dismantle the roots or motives, attitudes and emotions within the character or soul. Remember demons must have access through ignorance or agreement.

Our hearts and minds have been corrupted to see and believe things through distortions birthed in us through varied circumstances as well as through the sins committed by our ancestors. Familiar spirits know the sins that run through our family lines which give them legal right according to God's word to pressure one into committing the same sins with its curses or consequences.

Lord, The Lord God, compassionate and gracious, slow to anger and abounding in lovingkindness and truth who keeps lovingkindness, who forgives iniquity, transgression, and sin; yet He will by no means leave the guilty unpunished visiting the iniquity of fathers on the children and on the grandchildren to the third and fourth generations, Exodus 34: 6-7.

Sin can be described as the motive of the heart which leads to transgression or the unrighteous action committed. Iniquity are those sins and transgressions which run in one's family line. God forgives those who repent but the God of mercy is also a God of justice.

Repentance is the most powerful tool we have in spiritual warfare. It removes the legal right for Satan's attacks. Repentance is a willful choice through God's grace to see something as God sees it with a subsequent change of mind and action.

Father God calls us to identify with our ancestors' sins and repent on their behalf as well as our own. "If we confess our sins, and the sins of our fathers, and humble ourselves, He will remember His covenant." Leviticus 25: 40-42. "If we confess our sins, He is faithful and just to forgive us our sins and to cleanse us from all unrighteousness." 1 John 1:9.

TYPICAL RECURRING SINS OF FAMILIES

Abandonment: emotional or physical	Physical Infirmities
Abuse: emotional, physical, mental, sexual	Pride
Addictions	Rebellion
Anger, Rage, Violence	Rejection, Insecurity
Control, Manipulation	Religious Bondage, Cults
Divorce	Sexual Sin and Perversion
Fears of all kinds	Unbelief
Idolatry	Unworthiness, Low Self-Esteem, Inferiority
Money Extremes, Greed, Lack	Witchcraft, Occult, Satanism

FIVE (5) important steps or actions to take if you have opened a door to the occult or other sin(s) that gives the evil one legal access to bring demonic oppression:

1. REPENT - this is an act of your will to choose to turn from sin in thought and action with God's grace.
2. RENOUNCE - say out loud that you no longer want this in your life, and you are cutting ties to it.
3. FORGIVE - ask God to forgive you for the sin(s), forgive yourself or others which means you release any right to be angry or hold resentment then place the sin(s) on the cross.
4. RECEIVE GOD'S FORGIVENESS - actively receive God's promise to forgive you and to wash or cleanse you from all unrighteousness and to refresh you as you rest in His presence.
5. SEEK HELP - from an elder/pastor/minister should you need it.

PRAYER FOR RENOUNCING CURSED OBJECTS

Lord, I come to you about cursed objects and any demon infestation in my possessions, home, or workplace. I ask your forgiveness for having any such items in the precious name of Jesus. I understand that this is idolatry. Please forgive me.

Please show me any cursed objects, symbols, or demon infestation and spirits that need to be cast out. I will cast out the evil spirits out of my house in the precious name of Jesus.

I renounce any ties or expected benefits to having these items.

I receive your forgiveness according to your word that, "If we confess our sins, He is faithful and just to forgive us our sins and to cleanse us from all unrighteousness," 1 John 1:9.

Thank you for delivering me. Amen.

FORGIVENESS PRAYER FOR SINS OF ANCESTORS

As a child of God, purchased by the blood of the Lord Jesus Christ, I choose to confess and acknowledge the sins of my ancestors. I choose to forgive and release them and not to hold them accountable for each and every way that their sins have affected me.

I now renounce all of the sins of my ancestors and release myself from their effects, based on the finished work of Christ on the Cross.

Lord, I am sorry for all of the ways that I have entered into these same sins and allowed the curses to affect me. I ask You to forgive me for this and to wash me clean. I choose to receive Your forgiveness.

I affirm that I have been crucified with Jesus Christ and raised to walk in newness of life. On this basis, I announce to Satan and all his forces that Christ took upon Himself the curses and judgments due me. Thus I break every curse that has come upon me because of my ancestors. I also break all curses that have been released onto me by others. I also break all curses that I have spoken or thought about myself. I receive my freedom from every one of these curses.

Because of the above and because I have been delivered from the power of darkness and translated into the kingdom of God's dear Son, I cancel the legal rights of every demon sent to oppress me.

Because I have been raised up with Christ and now sit with Him in heavenly places, where I have a place as a member of God's family, I renounce and cancel each and every way that Satan and his demons may claim ownership of me. I cancel all dedications made by my ancestors or their descendants, including me and my descendants in the name of Jesus. I declare myself to be completely and eternally signed over to, owned by, and committed to, the Lord Jesus Christ.

All this I do based on the Truth revealed in the Word of God and in the Name and with the authority of my Lord and Savior, Jesus Christ. Amen!

(Forgiveness Prayer For Sins of Ancestors from <u>Restoring the Foundations</u> by Chester and Betsy Kylstra.)

REPENTANCE PRAYERS FOR OPENING DOORS TO DEMONIC OPPRESSION

Remember to be specific and name each occultic activity or sin individually and out loud.

1. Lord, I am choosing this day to repent from the following sin or occult activity: _____

2. Lord, I renounce and no longer want this occult activity or sin in my life and cut all ties to it: _____

3. Lord forgive me for participating in the following occult activity or sin: _____

4. Lord, I forgive _____ (anyone who introduced me to the following occult activities or participated in this sin with me if indicated).

5. Lord, I thank you for forgiving me as I place all these sins on the cross based on your word in 1John 1:9 which says, "If we confess our sins, he is faithful and just to forgive us our sins and to cleanse us from all unrighteousness."

6. Lord I now receive your forgiveness for these sins (pause and wait on the Holy Spirit as He cleanses your spirit, soul, and body from these sins).

7. Lord I now receive your refreshing for these sins that I have repented from according to your word which says, Repent ye therefore, and be converted, that your sins may be blotted out, when the times of refreshing shall come from the presence of the Lord, Acts 3:19.

4
ENCOUNTERING GOD

Christianity is not a set of rules of do's and don'ts to be accomplished by human effort. Christianity is a relationship with God which starts immediately upon our belief in and confession of Jesus Christ as Lord and Savior. We are given the Holy Spirit (third person of the Triune God) who indwells within us. Since Christianity is a relationship, it is established and fostered through communication. God speaks in multiple ways i.e. His Spirit and His Word, angels, audible voice, dreams, visions, miracles, creation, numbers, etc. so that we can know Him intimately. The Bible is filled with many who encountered God and were transformed.

"Who also hath made us able ministers of the new testament: not of the letter, but of the Spirit: for the letter killeth, but the Spirit giveth life," 2 Corinthians 3:6. "Jesus said to His Father, this is life eternal, that they might know thee, the only true God, and Jesus Christ, whom thou hast sent," John 17:3. A.W Tozer wrote in The Crucified Life : One important point many fail to understand that the Bible was never meant to replace God; rather, it was meant to lead us into the heart of God. Too many Christians stop with the text and never go on to experience the presence of God.

> *The Bible was never meant to replace God; rather, it was meant to lead us into the heart of God. Too many Christians stop with the text and never go on to experience the presence of God, A.W. Tozer.*

Can a human being who is constrained by the dimension of time relate to a God who is unrestrained by it? Since our souls and spirits are eternal then we may also be able to transcend the constraints of time and even matter when we fellowship with God through His Word and Spirit. God's Word is powerful and enables us to discern what is soul and what is spirit. The soul is our mind, will and emotions which is in touch with the natural world. The spirit is the portion of a human which is made alive to God and His Word when one becomes a follower of Jesus Christ. The spirit is the center of a person which is surrounded by their soul and their bodies. By faith in God's Word and by our spirit we can and do encounter God. We are to recognize what we encounter with God according to His Word, His character, and His attributes found in the Bible.

1. We can encounter God every time we read His Word and accept the reality of its contents by doing the following:
    - Read each section of it with the revelation that the Holy Spirit is within you to lead you to encounter the Son
    - Read it and choose to accept God's Word as truth to you personally.
    - Read it and believe that you are being transformed
    - Read it through the power of the Holy Spirit to change you from glory to glory.
    - Read it repenting of any sin identified

2. Here is an example of encountering God through the reading of His Word in Ephesians 3:17-19:

    <u>That Christ may dwell in your hearts through faith -</u> Meditate on the fact that He lives within you and turn your focus to Him through faith.

    <u>that you being rooted and grounded in love -</u> Wait on the Lord as you revel in the fact that you are rooted and grounded in the One who is Love. Believe as fact that you are rooted and grounded in love not fear. Encounter this Savior who loves you so much that His body was broken for you. Wait on Him to show you any area in your heart that does not believe this. Allow the Lord to speak His love into any area in your heart that needs to be healed or refreshed as you repent of unbelief.

    <u>may be able to comprehend with all the saints -</u> Ask God to give you a fresh understanding of the dimensions of His love for you and all His children through the Cross.

    <u>what is the width and length and depth and height, to know the love of Christ which passeth knowledge -</u> Encounter Him as the river of Living Water that runs so wide that it brings life to all of your body, soul, and spirit; Encounter Him as the height of an infinite heaven that has chosen to seat you with Him in heavenly places etc.

DEVOTION TO CHRIST

The Christian life is based on pure devotion to Jesus Christ. Draw nigh to God and He will draw nigh to you. Daily devotion to the One who saved you from being eternally separated from Him and all that is good. Being devoted means you love that person, activity, or item very much. I know of people who are devoted to their ministries, jobs, families, financial portfolios, even God's blessings. But did you know God wants you to be devoted to Him first. He is a jealous God. Why because He is insecure? No, because He made you to only find fulfillment in a relationship with Him. He created mankind to walk in unbroken glory- filled relationship just like He did with Adam and Eve. Devotion to God isn't just

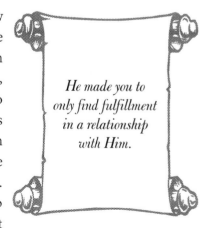

He made you to only find fulfillment in a relationship with Him.

about how much time you spend with Him but it is all about God. Jesus Christ and God, the Father are real personal beings and we can relate to them through the Person of the Holy Spirit. You will grow in love with the Lord as you commune with Him through acknowledging His Presence, through studying, meditating on His Word and applying His Word in your life.

DRAWN TO ENTER HIS PRESENCE

I read a book many years ago, The Practice of the Presence of God and found myself very frustrated after reading it. Many of the books written by wonderful saints of old did not always explain the how to's of their spiritual disciplines. God's will for us is to "be able to comprehend with all saints what is the breadth, and length, and depth, and height and to know the love of Christ which passeth knowledge, that ye might be filled with all the fulness of God," Ephesians 3:18-19. Love is not just a concept to be measured and grasped by the believer's natural mind but as the word says, it passeth knowledge or it transcends knowledge gained from the intellect alone. Love is the Father, Son, and Holy Spirit (One God) who is meant to be encountered.

The more I meditated on Jesus, the Blood and the power and efficacy of the Cross in the book of Hebrews the more I was being drawn to enter God's presence. God's word says, having boldness to enter into the holiest by the blood of Jesus, Hebrews 10:19. One day in 2005 while in prayer and by faith I said to God "I am coming in." By faith and in my heart/spirit I went into encountering His presence. By faith I believed that I could enter the Holiest of Holies and I entered God's presence. I did not imagine God or what he would be like, I just trusted in His Word that said I could enter where He resides. Once there I was overwhelmed by sensing Father God's provision and care and the rest of the day, I was charged to give things away to people.

OLD AND NEW TESTAMENT FORESHADOWING OF ENCOUNTERING GOD

The Old Testament gives us a foreshadowing of man entering the Holy of Holies in the temple through the many rituals and bloody sacrifices required. There are many individuals who experienced and saw God's glory and the activities in the throne room and the heavenlies in the Old and New Testament. Here are a few: Jacob who dreamt of angels ascending and descending and God spoke in Genesis 28-12; God spoke to Moses out of the burning bush in Exodus 3:2-6; Aaron, Nadab, Abihu saw God on the mountain in Exodus 24:9-10; Micaiah tells of seeing the Lord on His throne in 1Kings 22:19; Isaiah saw the Lord sitting on a throne in Isaiah 6:1-3; Ezekiel saw that the heavens were opened and saw visions of God in Ezekiel 1:1; Daniel saw the Ancient of Days being seated in Daniel 7:9-14; Stephen saw the glory of God and Jesus standing at the right hand of God in Acts 7: 55-56; Paul heard Jesus speaking to him in Acts 26:14-16; and John saw a door open in heaven and saw God on the throne in Revelation 4:1-11. Now, as a believer in Christ we are the temple of God. God desires to have his throne room in our hearts.

King David in the Old Testament was a good example of someone who practiced the presence of God. He spent hours as a shepherd communing with his Lord. David experienced God the Father and God the Pre-Incarnate Son when he said, "The Lord (Yahweh) says to my Lord (Adonai), sit at my right hand until I make your enemies your footstool," Psalm 110:1. David also penned other words on the presence of God. He wrote in Psalm 16:11, "In your presence is fullness of joy, in your right hand there are pleasures forever."

The New Testament or Covenant which is far better than the old tells us that because of the blood sacrifice of Jesus Christ we can boldly (with confidence) enter into the throne of grace as well as the Holy of Holies.

ACKNOWLEDGING GOD'S PRESENCE

Acknowledging God's presence is the spiritual act of turning your attention to focus on Him who lives within you. "God is love; and he that dwelleth in love dwelleth in God, and God in him," 1John 4:16. In doing so, you are bypassing those things that distract you. Acknowledging His Presence will enable you to commune or relate to God through your soul (mind, will emotions) and spirit. It is a heart activity which can be done at any time or in any place. We believe in our hearts as cited in Romans 10:9, "That if though confess with thy mouth the Lord Jesus, and shalt believe in thine heart that God hath raised him from the dead though shalt be saved." We are called to walk intimately with the Lord just as Adam and Eve and many others have done over the centuries as previously discussed in Chapter 3.

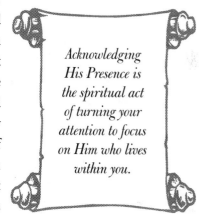

Acknowledging His Presence is the spiritual act of turning your attention to focus on Him who lives within you.

REST FROM LIFE'S BURDENS

Jesus said, "come unto me all ye that labor and are heavy laden and I will give you rest," Matthew 11:28. Consider all that you do in life as labor. Come to Him daily before your activities, (i.e., praying, going to work or school) and receive His rest. Jesus gives you what no one else can give – rest from the burden of sin or struggling to do the right thing. He will lift the weights of your day, your heart, and your life if you will but come to Him. Learn from Him for He is meek and lowly. He had all the same power and glory as His Father yet He leaned on God the Father and God the Holy Spirit to accomplish all that He did in His short 33-year life span. We too can lean on the Spirit of God to accomplish what we are called to do during our day.

INTIMATE TIME WITH THE KING OF KINGS

Remember we are all unique and you will develop your way to acknowledge God's presence and to live a life devoted to Him. This is not a formula but a relationship which can vary from day to day.

Remember intimacy with God takes time and commitment. I do not come to God during this time with prayers and petitions etc. I come simply to be with Him and allow God to be my Lord. My greatest need is to know, love and worship Him. He alone is the reward and the one you and I really require. We were made for Him.

My greatest need is to know, love and worship Him. He alone is the reward and the one you and I really require. We were made for Him.

Recommendations:

- Assume a comfortable position in a quiet place if possible.
- Put on Christian worship music, (i.e., Julie True, Kimberly & Alberto Rivera, etc.)
- By faith, knowing that Christ's Spirit lives within the believer, acknowledge or enter His presence by turning from self-focus to Jesus-focus.
- I use the many scriptures that tell what the throne room is like (e.g. Isaiah 6:1) and what God is like as they are more real than what we experience here in the natural. I envision the Lord high and lifted up or as Jesus standing before me. Jesus is God but He is also a man. I have a wonderful book with the names of God and will meditate on one of His names or a bible verse that describes God to encounter Him.
- Once I sense God's <u>peace and presence</u>, I bow to Him in worship. His presence produces instant joy and peace for me and I have learned to be still and know that He is God. This can also be done instantly anywhere you are by focusing on the Lord.
- Should you have difficulty sensing God's peace and presence try the following:
  a. <u>First examine yourself for any sin</u> in your life then confess, repent, renounce and ask for forgiveness or forgive anyone who has wronged you. "Therefore repent and return, so that your sins may be wiped away in order that times of refreshing may come from the presence of the Lord", Acts 3:19. Allow the Lord to wash over your mind and body and receive His forgiveness and sense His refreshing you. Do not be in a hurry to leave this wonderful time of recharging that the Lord promises to His children.
  b. <u>Cast all your cares onto Him for He cares for you</u>. Note: this is an act of humility. God gives His grace to the humble. Example: I will literally envision any negative emotion or experience in a box or in my hand and drop it at the feet of Jesus. There are times when it takes me awhile to deal with my emotions or upsets in life before I can sense God's peace and presence. Working through these things is especially important and healing. I cast all my cares onto Him daily and even throughout the day as cares, worries etc. arise. He is our refuge in times of trouble, so I also envision myself in a restful position surrounded

by Him when I discern the enemy's attacks on my thoughts, emotions, and body. God's word is powerful and real. We really by faith can run into Him.

ABIDING RELATIONSHIP

Abiding in Christ and His word will produce the light, love, and holiness of Christ within you. The more you become aware of His presence and draw near to Him throughout the day, even if only for seconds, the greater your abiding in Him will grow. Study, meditate, memorize, speak, and do His word because you love Him and want to know and honor your lovely Savior and Lord.

The Holy Spirit within you will always lead you to Jesus and the truth of His Word.

Loving God can be a feeling, but it is much more than that. Jesus himself declared that the love that His Father has for Him will be in us. The love that the Father has for the Son is manifested in bringing Him glory and honor.

Declare along with Jesus that the same love the Father has for the Son will be in you.
You will have many choices all day long to choose life (God's Word) or death (sin).
Choose life through the power of His Spirit.

Remember that being a Christian is firstly about relationship with God. Repentance or confessing sin keeps this relationship close and under the shadow of His wings or covering. We are to be motivated by love for the one who first loved us, died for us while still yet sinners, and repeatedly has mercy on us in our weakness. "If a man love me, he will keep my words," John 14:23. God shows us the way by stressing the word love before obedience. Attempting to obey God with human effort alone and without loving gratitude and grace found in relationship can lead to frustration, anger, and failure. Honest, daily abiding communication with God leads to abundant life.

We have a free will. Our flesh as Paul says does not like to do God's will at times. We are commanded to forgive at all times but our flesh may argue back to God, "Did you hear what that person just said to me?" So, one may find themselves in a struggle to choose to forgive. If one chooses life which is to: love (do what is best for the other person),walk in light (God's Word), live in holiness (committed relationship to God), then he or she will be blessed and remain abiding in Christ as His Word abides in him or her.

If one chooses death (sin) their soul has now stepped out of abiding in Christ and out of the shadow of His wings where He promises protection, spiritual growth, and fruit. One is to go to the Lord in a time of need for His grace to choose God's righteousness or doing things His Way. When dealing with hurts, negative emotions (i.e., anger, anxiety, fear, depression, frustration, jealousy etc.) practice the same steps of getting into His presence and ask the Lord if there is any hidden sin (i.e., unforgiveness attached to the painful emotions or unbelief or mistrust of God himself. Ask yourself, if God says I do not have to be anxious for anything then what is it I am not able to trust Him for? Why not?

We are in a good fight of faith and the more you know God, His Word, and His absolute Goodness the stronger your faith will become. Maturing as a Christian is a process, but it will take even longer if you do not spend time with Him, hearing and doing His word. Submit to God and resist the enemy. It is so much easier to submit to a God who you know is always good and loves you through His Word and in encountering Him.

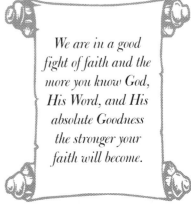

We are in a good fight of faith and the more you know God, His Word, and His absolute Goodness the stronger your faith will become.

"Likewise reckon ye also yourselves to be dead indeed unto sin but alive unto God through Jesus Christ our Lord," Romans 6:11. Yes, our feelings can be very overwhelming and powerful at times, but once you choose to submit negative thoughts, emotions, and turning from sinful actions to God, resisting the enemy becomes easier.

DERAILING FEAR

The times that we are living in are perilous. Men's hearts are going to fail them for fear according to Luke 21:26. We are all going to need to deal with fear in this hour. Fellowshipping with The One Who is Love, Peace and Joy is a prescription to defeat fear in this hour. You have instant access to God because of the blood of Jesus and the Word. His Word says, perfect love casteth out fear. God Himself is perfect love so believe Him to cast out your fear.

MY TESTIMONY

I had skin cancer (minor lesion) in 2020. Nowadays you get the results of your tests on a computer portal. I was afraid to look at the follow-up procedure results. Then I thought well I had better do what I am teaching others. So, I went and sat with the Lord. It was not long before the fear was gone and I was able to look at the results. The Holy Spirit revealed to me during that time that everything would be fine.

Yes, everything was fine but the fear I was facing was real. While spending time in His presence the Lord cast out my fear. I am still rejoicing over our faithful God as He looks over His word to perform it.

RECOMMENDED ACTIONS TO DEVELOPING INTIMACY WITH THE LORD

Remember length of time spent with God depends on many factors such as desire, schedule, health, obligations, etc.

1. Daily Dependence - Realizing your absolute dependence on God to live the Christian life.

2. Daily Devotion - a) Putting God first in your life before other activities and throughout the day by acknowledge or practicing His presence even if only for 5 minutes. b) Reading, studying, thinking, or meditating on His Word. c) Reading books others have written on their devotional lives. d) Worshipping God. e) Knowing that true fulfillment in life only comes through a relationship with the Lord. f) Gratitude toward God.

3. Daily Quietness - Waiting on the Lord in quietness allowing God to lead. Allowing Him to heal you, refresh you, fill you, reveal truth and Himself to you.

4. Daily Abiding - Choosing to live out of a) Christ's light (His Word), b) Christ's love (thinking of others first) c) Christ's holiness – devotion to Christ and His righteousness

5. Daily Honest Communication - Sharing your thoughts, feelings, hurts, questions, doubts etc. with the Lord as they arise.

6. Daily Confessing of Sin and Repentance - Examine yourself, and then confess and repent for any heart attitudes, actions, speech, unforgiveness etc. that is contrary to God's word and will for you.

7. Daily Receiving God's Forgiveness and Refreshing - After a time of self- examination, receive His forgiveness and refreshing found in His Presence.

8. Daily Submitting to God and Resisting the Enemy - Set your mind and heart each morning to obey the Lord and resist the temptation to choose to walk in darkness or Satan's kingdom.

5
ORIGINS OF DEPRESSION, ANXIETY, ANGER

The origin of our emotional problems to some degree can be traced to a spiritual root of unbelief in God's goodness and the truth of His Word. Perhaps then, depression, anxiety and anger are not the root of one's misery but may rise out of one's unbelief toward God, one's pride and one's bent towards self. "God is not a man that He should lie, neither the son of man that He should repent: hath He said, and shall He not do it? Or hath he spoken and shall He not make it good?" Numbers 23:19.

SATAN EXALTS SELF

Satan 's 5 "I will" statements: 1) "I will ascend into heaven" 2) "I will exalt my throne above the stars of God" 3) "I will sit also upon the mount of the congregation" 4) "I will ascend above the heights of the clouds" 5) I will be like the most high" found in Isaiah 14:13-14 mirrors the bent in Satan's heart and subsequently in man to exalt self above God. This is the sin of pride. You may be saying to yourself, " What does pride have to do with depression, anxiety, and anger?" Well, one chooses to elevate one's thoughts, emotions, attitudes, understandings, agreements, desires, actions, etc. over the truth of God's perfect character and His Word. Does one have understanding or awareness of doing this? Not always, but God says in Hosea 4:6, My people are destroyed for lack of knowledge. God does not ignore our ignorance.

When I first heard a prominent woman minister say that depression was self-pity, I was quite offended. It took me awhile to admit that self-had been my focus. Another time I was upset at myself for failing and sinning. God gently impressed the following thought to me: "Cheryl, what made you think there was nothing wrong with you." I knew immediately that He meant my self-condemnation was pride. If there was nothing wrong with us then Jesus died in vain.

When I first heard a prominent woman minister say that depression was self-pity, I was quite offended.

It can be very painful to hear anything negative about self if one has been casualty to rejection, abandonment, and subsequent self-rejection. A stronghold or mindset of rejection/self-rejection is constructed with lies and demonic influences to protect oneself from further pain. When a physical wound is filled with the bodies' own defense mechanisms it may be necessary to incise and drain it for the tissue to heal. This analogy can apply to a mental stronghold. In order for it to be healed one needs to acknowledge wrong thinking and self-focus. Mental strongholds are thinking patterns, belief systems, attitudes and motives that oppose the truth of God's character and His Word.

God's pattern for emotional healing starts with humility. Humility is not self-deprecating thoughts and speech but a heart set on God and His will and purposes in the earth. Jesus was our perfect example. "Humble ourselves in the sight of the Lord and He shall lift you up," James 4:10. "Not my will but thine be done," Luke 22:42.

The secret of finding blessedness in everything is simply letting God have His own way and making your will the reverberation of His.

LIES AND HALF-TRUTHS

The enemy uses his legal rights gained through our ancestor's sins, our sins, and the sins of those around us to erode our faith and trust in God. He uses all of these factors which include lies or half-truths based on ancestor's sins and hurtful or traumatic experiences in our lives which when repeated reinforce the falsehoods. These falsehoods also come from the natural mind of mankind. They seem logical and appealing but they have the stench of worldly standards of man, such as concepts of worldly success, popularity, happiness etc. Lies believed or unbelief of God's perfect character and His Word give demons legal right to oppress. The lies or our unbelief shut off God's hand to bless us, since "Without faith it is impossible to please God because anyone who comes to Him must believe that He exists and that He rewards those who earnestly seek Him." Hebrews 11:6.

Hopefully, you can see that the enemy and our very own fallen nature give rise to unbelief.

Hopefully, you can see that the enemy and our very own fallen nature give rise to unbelief. God does not reward unbelief or lack of faith. We then in turn may become angry at God for not blessing us or answering our prayers. This sequence can morph into blatant denial of a good God and His very existence and the enemy loves it. He has succeeded by sowing division between man and God. Matthew 17:20, "And Jesus said unto them, Because of your unbelief: for verily I say unto you, if ye have faith as a grain of mustard seed ye shall say to this mountain, Remove hence to yonder place, and it shall remove, and nothing shall be impossible to you."

REPLACING LIES WITH THE TRUTH OF GOD'S WORD

The repenting and healing of the roots of these ungodly mindsets opens the door for believing God's character and His Word. One's heart if filled with lies about God, self, others, and life has great difficulty being filled with the truth. These lies and the cause for them when uprooted and healed are to be replaced with the Word of God.

EXAMPLE: Lie based on being left and ignored by one's father.

Lie believed: I am alone in the world and have no one who cares for me. God is like my dad he won't be there for me.

Truth: "I am accepted in the beloved," Ephesians 1:6 ; "That Christ may dwell in your hearts by faith; that ye, being rooted and grounded in love," Ephesians 3:17.

This is the core of inner healing and deliverance. It is the removing of unbelief in God's perfect character and His perfect Word. It is the repenting and healing of the unbelieving heart to be free to agree with God.

KINGDOM OF GOD IS AT HAND (REPENT AND BELIEVE)

The sins of unbelief and pride (our tendency toward self) are fortresses that are built on Satan's purposeful seduction along with our willful choice which disrupts our faith in the one true God and His Word.

The Spirit of God works upon one's heart to reestablish God's order. Jesus Christ of Nazareth came to restore the kingdom of God. The kingdom of God is God's spiritual rule over the hearts and lives of those who willingly submit to His authority. Jesus preached that repentance is necessary to be a part of the kingdom of God.

I entered the kingdom of God when I repented and was born again in 1985. Many things due to sin in my life kept me from fully believing God and His Word. There are great benefits to believing God! Experiential knowledge of the kingdom of God which is righteousness, peace and joy in the Holy Spirit are but a few.

I retired from full-time work in 2016 which left me time to hike and pray. I prayed in the Spirit while hiking and one day I asked the Lord, "what am I praying about?" The Lord impressed on me that He was putting things in His order. Even after all those years of praying and reading the word and experiencing miracles I had to realize God still was not number one in my life. For God to be primary in my life would be God's order. He is a jealous God and will burn out everything that we put ahead of Him in our lives. When He does, it is ultimately to our benefit and to our health and happiness.

6
BLOODY VICTORY OVER STRONGHOLDS

A stronghold is a mental and spiritual fortress or wall that is created on deception and arguments against the character and Word of God. It is formulated through hurtful memories, trauma, curses, lies, and half-truths reinforced through demonic entities. The Blood of Jesus overcame these mental strongholds which can produce depression, anxiety, anger and more. When you think of Jesus, think of His blood and all that it accomplished for you. When the enemy sends a fiery dart of unbelief or arguments against the Word of God it passes through the shield of the blood, which destroys its poisonous effect.

We as Christians have been given the most powerful weapons to change our beliefs, characters, attitudes, behavior and subsequently our earthly and eternal destinies. We are saved from the sins of self-focus in order to live the abundant life that Christ died to give us. This abundant life is God centered. Anything less than God being the focus is doomed to fail. "They overcame by the Blood of the Lamb, Word of their Testimony and they did not love their lives even unto death," Revelation 12:11.

> *We as Christians have been given the most powerful weapons to change our beliefs, characters, attitudes, behavior and subsequently our earthly and eternal destinies.*

In the garden of Gethsemane, Jesus Christ being both fully human and fully God anguished over anticipating the forces of Satan and His followers coming against Him through physical restraints, shame, mocking, bloody torture, and an excruciating death. Jesus was made to be sin with all of its' crushing guilt and vileness for us. Can you imagine the kind of severe anxiety He must have experienced in order to sweat drops of blood?

Around the sweat glands are bundles of blood vessels that constrict with extreme anxiety. Once the anxiety passes the blood vessels dilate and the blood flows from the sweat glands. Fear is the root of many physical and emotional problems. Jesus conquered every vestige of fear known to mankind in the Garden of Gethsemane because of His great love for us.

Demons of abandonment, anger, death, despair, fear, hatred, rejection, etc. were attacking Him. Jesus defeated everything that the enemy could hurl against us through the shedding of His blood.

He dealt with His own free will when choosing to submit to the Father's plan of salvation. Notice the difference in Jesus' submissive "I will" statements from Satan's self-aggrandizing statements. Jesus says three times in Luke 22:44, "Nevertheless not as I will, but as thou wilt." Jesus's statements were Father-God focused. Satan's "I will" statements were Satan or self-focused. Jesus conquered self-exaltation, entitlement, pride, and rebellion for you and me. He overcame the injustice of becoming the sinless substitution for a world who deserves death and destruction for their rejection of God and His sacrificial Lamb.

Jesus overcame shame, fear, and control, when he allowed the soldiers to repeatedly mock Him, pluck out His beard and keep his hands tied behind His back to control Him and to display His human weakness. He overcame the blindness to sin that Satan places on unbelieving hearts when He allowed the solders to blindfold and strike Him.

The Old Testament law in Exodus15:26 stipulated that the Israelites were to diligently listen for God's voice in order to keep His commandments. Keeping God's commandments would bless them with good health. Jesus fulfilled this law perfectly through His life and death which provides healing for God's people as stated in 1 Peter 2:24: "by whose stripes you were healed," and Isaiah 53:5: "But for our transgressions, He was bruised for our iniquities, the chastisement for our peace was upon Him and by His stripes we are healed."

He overcame all sins of the flesh (Galatian 5:19-21) when His flesh was violently torn, causing bleeding and great pain due to His exposed nerve endings during the Roman scourging. Jesus overcame the desire to have man's approval more than God's approval through the crowning of thorns which He endured with pain and mocking from the soldiers. He took the mockery Christians would face for believing in Him.

He overcame rebellion when He was nailed to the cross by refusing to call legions of angels to rescue Him. Jesus overcame abandonment when He called out to His Father, "Why have Thou forsaken me?" He no longer experienced His father's presence or approval while dying, because His Father could not look upon sin. God made Him who had no sin to be sin for us, so that in Him we might become the righteousness of God," 2 Corinthians 5:21. How many of us have been so discouraged or depressed due to our circumstances that we wonder how God could be for us if this is happening to us? Jesus knows all and He overcame everything that can come against us.

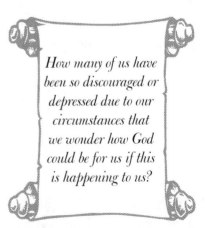

How many of us have been so discouraged or depressed due to our circumstances that we wonder how God could be for us if this is happening to us?

He destroyed the power of all sin through the shedding of His perfect sacrificial blood. "And the blood of Jesus Christ His Son cleanseth us from all sin," 1 John 1:7.

Knowing what Christ has done for you will enable you to believe the power in the weapon of his blood. You are washed in His blood, and that enables you to receive and believe in His victory and your freedom to walk in it.

DEPRESSION

Depression or its close relative self-pity drive one's thoughts to focus on oneself. The reality is that depression gives people a heightened sense of self-consciousness. In general people with depression tend to think about themselves, examine their personalities, real or perceived failures, and contemplate their feelings more than non-depressed people. Depression is also a spirit that runs in families and will exert pressure on an individual to respond to life with persistent moods of sadness or heaviness.

ANXIETY, FEAR AND WORRY

Anxiety, fear, and worry are associated feelings founded on unbelief in God's perfect character and His Word. One believes that God cannot be trusted to provide, protect, prevail in their lives and that they must accomplish these things on their own based on life's experiences. It is self-reliance undergirded by pride or the insistence that "I can do this on my own."

Experiences with rejection and failure can cast a big shadow on a human being's heart. Anxiety especially at an early age, whether inherited through a spirit of fear that runs in one's family or through traumatic life events, opens the door for many maladaptive behaviors. One of those maladaptive human responses can be anger.

ANGER

Unrighteous anger is founded on self-importance and entitlement as deemed by one's own summary judgment. It can be seen in the attitude that I should always have what I want or what I believe I deserve, and never be hurt or slighted by anyone. Anger can also be a learned behavioral response through authority figures such as our parents, along with a spirit that operates through one's ancestral line.

Anger which often follows fear (a threat or perceived danger) is a mechanism to restore a sense of control back to an individual. Control behaviors may be displayed in addictions, violence, manipulation, passive aggressive behaviors, witchcraft, and denial.

Our problem is we do not believe God and His Word. He says that we can do all things through Christ who strengthens us. Literally, we have the ability through the power of the Holy Spirit to do all that God says we can do.

Ask God to show you why you do not believe this verse or any of the other 31,102 verses in the Bible. We are trying to get to the root of our unbelief so that we can live the abundant life that Christ died to give us. The abundant life is a life submitted to His rulership through faith in the God who loves us.

ROOTS OF DEPRESSION, ANXIETY, AND ANGER

1. The sins of our ancestors can result in generational curses. These curses are a consequence of unbroken strongholds or ungodly mindsets passed through one's lineage. An example would be that your great grandparents, grandparents, parents, and other family members struggled with depression, anxiety, or anger. Demons can be passed down the family tree through this type of curse. Jesus became a curse for us so that we can live free of these curses but like all of God's benefits and gifts, this freedom must be received and appropriated.

2. Self-curses can be defeatist beliefs, or negative agreements with your life circumstances, emotions, or past experiences. Here are some examples: "I always feel depressed during the winter months or before my menses.;" "My depression is always there;" "I always feel anxious when I have to do something new;" "They always make me angry." God's word says life and death are in the power of the tongue, meaning that the words that you speak about yourself contain power that can influence your life. Curses or negative statements or ill wishes made toward us by others i.e., witches, warlocks, Satanists, or especially by those in authority over us such as a father saying, "you are stupid," can have a lifelong effect on us if not broken and dealt with.

3. Lies we believe about God, self, or others can come from soul wounds which are incurred in the mind, will, and emotions. Soul wounds cripple our ability to experience God. Lies believed can develop from trauma, rejection, abandonment, the world's teachings, philosophies, family beliefs or even unintentional parental teaching that suppresses emotions or ideas, etc. These lies or false beliefs need to be identified using God's Word, Holy Spirit and possibly help from a Christian minister or mentor. Examples would be, "God blesses others but not me," or "no one will love me," or "people just use me." You fell as a child and it hurt, but your parent told you it did not hurt. This opens the door for the lie that you cannot trust your perception or understanding of life.

4. Broken hearts or soul/spirit wounds can develop as the result of the sins of ancestors such as verbal, sexual, physical abuse, rejection, and abandonment. Rejection is being told that you are not good enough. Abandonment is being told that you are worthless.

5. A soul tie is an emotional or physical bond with someone that eventually forms a spiritual attachment. It is an invisible cord that ties you to another person. These can either be Godly soul ties or ungodly soul ties. The physical/emotional bond can come through healthy, Godly physical/emotional connection with family, your spouse, friends etc. Ungodly soul

ties can be formed with family, friends, a domineering authority, abusive relationships and can result in your feeling controlled, manipulated, dominated, fearful and angry. Ungodly soul ties develop in immoral relationships, excessive reliance on other people for approval or an unhealthy sense of identity. Holding anger or a judgment toward another or infatuation with a famous person can produce an ungodly soul tie. These ties need to be broken in order to bring down the strongholds or ungodly mindsets and structures, along with driving out the demons that reinforce the structures.

6. Anxiety can cause depression as stated in Proverbs 12:25: "Heaviness in the heart of man maketh it stoop," which means that anxiety or worry weighs down one's heart leading to depression. When one is anxious, one tends to think about a problem excessively which can lead to feelings of failure, which opens the door for depression.

7. Physical or mental disabilities, illnesses, grief, losses, isolation, etc. can lead to anxiety, depression, and anger.

8. Fear and rejection open the door for anger.

9. Unforgiveness, judgments, witchcraft, occult, New Age involvement, unconfessed sin and broken vows can open the doors to depression, anxiety and anger as discussed in previous chapters.

Knowing God through His Word and His Presence is key to conquering anxiety, depression, and anger. We were made for love, acceptance and purpose in life and God your creator has it all for you. The following chapters will give you a roadmap to the life God intended for you. This roadmap is founded on an active relationship with God which will produce a healed heart and soul.

7
GOD'S LOVE NEVER FAILS

Depression ran in my family. My grandmother, my mom, and my brother all suffered from depression. A picture of myself at four years old revealed the spirit of heaviness or depression on my face. But like the woman with the issue of blood who had heard that the healer Jesus was going to be near, I heard God was showing up at a church in Toronto, Canada in January of 1994. I was desperate and had suffered with depression since my childhood. I had read a book by Mike Bickle entitled Passion for Jesus. After reading it I told the Lord, I don't feel this way about You, I am not passionate about You," and at the time I found the book nauseating. Again, my thoughts and feelings were clouded because of my hurts and relationship with my parents but especially my dad. My heart believed that God was powerful like my dad when he punched me or was verbally raging, and that He also was unkind, a poor provider and distant like my dad.

The Lord impressed on me three times to ask for the Baptism in Fire when I arrived at the church in Toronto. I wasn't even quite sure what the Baptism in Fire was, as I had never heard anyone teach on it. One of the prayer team members asked me what I wanted. I told him the Baptism in Fire. He asked me if, I was sure. I said yes, and he said, "Lord, give her the desire of her heart."

What followed was a miraculous deliverance in 1994 from a mental stronghold of depression and self-pity while in the Spirit at the Toronto Airport Christian Fellowship. I experienced Jesus as absolute love and goodness, and I felt that each cell of my body was only fulfilled in Him. I left the church that night delivered from depression and found that I was passionately in love with Jesus. I could hardly bear the pain of leaving His presence.

Looking back on that miraculous event, it became clear to me that when I encountered God as love, my heart was delivered and healed from the lies that I believed about Him.

It is the knowledge and the encountering of Him as love that will heal you, too. Yes, you can pray all the prayers in this book and other Christian books which are powerful and will give you a measure of freedom in Christ, but it is the on-going knowing and encountering of Him as love that will truly heal you. It is the knowing of this God who loves you which will root you and ground you in Him. His love did for me in one hour what nine years of trying to heal myself through reading and studying His Word with an unbelieving heart could not do. The Baptism in Fire progressively burned-out idolatrous desires in me. Jesus has since then become the true desire of my heart. John the Baptist said of Jesus,

"I indeed baptize you with water unto repentance, but He that cometh after me is mightier than I, whose shoes I am not worthy to bear; he shall baptize you with the Holy Ghost, and with fire," Matthew 3:11.

POST DELIVERANCE INSIGHTS

There were many days in the beginning of learning to remain free from depression and self-pity that I would repeatedly walk around and say out loud, "I will not feel sorry for myself." I had well over thirty plus years of struggling with depression. Following my miraculous deliverance from it, I decided that I was not going back again. It takes energy to become and stay depressed. You must think negative thoughts about God, self, or others, listen to sad music, watch sad movies, or shows etc. I can use that same energy to change my thoughts, words, and behavior.

I began to tell myself that depression will not help anything get better in my life, so why choose to be depressed? I can feel and think more positive thoughts with negative circumstances just as well as be depressed (which I hate) with those same negative circumstances.

EMOTIONS ARE A CHOICE

Chronic negative emotions such as anger, fear and depression are signposts to broken areas in our hearts. Our inability to trust God's character and His Word seem very reasonable if one has experienced numerous mild to severe hurts in life. One of my favorite Bible verses is Jeremiah 17:7-8, "Blessed is the man who trusteth in the Lord and whose hope the Lord is." This implies that when we trust God with our lives and futures, he honors that trust through blessings. Trusting God produces a positive emotional state. It is much easier to trust God once the emotional roadblocks have been dismantled through counseling and ministry, (see Chapters 8-12). A book was written years ago entitled Happiness

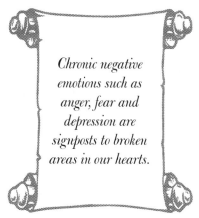

Chronic negative emotions such as anger, fear and depression are signposts to broken areas in our hearts.

is a Choice and I genuinely believe this. I practiced smiling (no matter how I felt) throughout the day. Try this, it really works. I took self-pity thoughts captive unto Christ and would stop thinking about myself altogether. Instead of feeling sorry for myself, I would pray, call others, or do something nice for someone else. We have control over our feelings, emotions, and behavior with the power of the

Holy Spirit. You may be saying to yourself right about now, that you cannot control how you feel. God's Word says otherwise. You can choose to control anger, and then rejoice and be glad. "He that is slow to anger is better than the mighty; and he that ruleth his spirit than he that taketh a city," Proverbs 16:32. "This is the day the Lord has made; I will rejoice, and I will be glad in it," Psalm 118: 24. Spoiler alert, you can even choose to trust God.

CHANGING FOCUS

While minimizing self-focus and growing toward God focus, I began to change. "Seek first the kingdom of God and His righteousness and all these things shall be added unto thee," Matthew 6: 33. As I sought the Lord first and focused on others, our faithful God met all of my needs according to His riches in glory.

It is difficult to be miserable while abiding in Christ and His presence. It is His love that will heal your heart and keep you in His perfect peace. It is His magnificence, glory, love, mercy, grace, joy, etc. that He desires to enthrall you with. Don't settle for worldly substitutes when what your heart has been fashioned for can only be realized in Him. Relationship with God takes time, effort, and diligence but He is worth it all. "Draw nigh to God, and he will draw nigh to you," James 4:8.

His will is that you know Him in the midst of life's difficulties. His will is that you trust Him as He comforts, strengthens, and gives you hope in your trials. He longs to show Himself mighty to you if you will rest in Him and believe in His goodness and His Word. He is faithful to look over His Word to perform it. The Holy Spirit who resides within you is the reason you can be strong when you feel weak. He is the Spirit of Power, the Spirit of Love, The Spirit of a Sound Mind, 2 Timothy 1:7.

KNOWING PERFECT LOVE REALLY CASTS OUT FEAR

The Holy Spirit was continuing His beautiful work in my heart. He graced me to begin putting Him first in my life. Do I do this perfectly every day? No, but most days now He is consuming my thoughts and desires. When God says, "be anxious for nothing," Philippians 4:6; "perfect love casts out fear," 1 John 4:18; and "cast all of your cares,"1 Peter 5:7, then I have no reason not to believe Him, right? It is a very fearful thing not to trust God. Who else is there to go to for help? God was draining my heart of unbelief as He was becoming my chief desire.

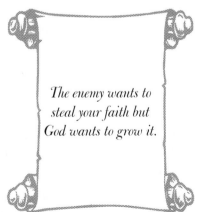

The enemy wants to steal your faith but God wants to grow it.

Surely this God who is love and loves me, would help me each time I asked. One can rest knowing that He is helping. Let's park here a minute. When you do not feel or see the help you are asking for, you may fall into the trap of being disappointed, angry or you may lose your faith. Remember, it is impossible to please God without faith. The enemy wants to steal your faith but God wants to grow it. Growing faith takes time and testing. "Knowing that the testing of your faith produces patience," James 1:3.

The more you know Him the more you will trust Him. You will have bold faith and confidence in the One who came, suffered, died, and rose again so you would be an overcomer in this life! The revelation of God is the true antidote to fear. Knowing the One Who is perfect love, will cast out fear. Fear is a demonic spirit. When you submit to believing and trusting God, you can "resist the devil, and he will flee." James 4:7.

All the roadblocks to trusting God are to be demolished and replaced with faith in God's goodness and the truth of His Word. Fear is the lack of knowledge of perfect love. This is not just head knowledge of the Bible verse. It is rather being in close relationship with perfect love who is God the Father, Son, and Holy Spirit.

Fear will keep you from your destiny and purpose in this life. Moses was kept out of the Promised Land because He was afraid and did not believe God's Word to speak to the rock, so He struck the rock twice. The rock symbolized Christ our rock. He failed to put His trust in God's Word and God's goodness to provide life-giving water to His people. God's goodness was to begin a new chapter with the Israelites in the promised land. His purpose was to lay a foundation of belief and faith in God's Word and His abilities to conquer the giants in the land. So, God kept Moses from entering the Promised Land due to his unbelief as the leader of the people.

Your unbelief and fear will keep you out of God's full purpose and God's call on your life too! You are in the New Covenant with greater promises. Jesus is "the author and the finisher of our faith," Hebrews 12:2. He is doing a mighty and effective work in you!

OVERCOMING UNRIGHTEOUS (SINFUL) ANGER

"Wherefore my beloved brethren, let every man be swift to hear, slow to speak, slow to wrath. For the wrath of man worketh not the righteousness of God," James 1:19-20.

Wrath or anger can be either righteous or unrighteous. Righteous anger is when we witness an offense against God or His Word and react. Unrighteous anger seeks to hurt or to lash out. It is not based on love, kindness, and respect. Feelings of anger are not sin until acted upon. God cautions us to not let the enemy have a foothold by allowing our feelings of anger and resentment to simmer or to let the sun go down before resolving the issue.

Chronic anger can cause negative physical effects. It can indirectly lead to cardiovascular disease, migraines, fatigue, and it can reduce the immune system's ability to defend against infections.

Anger can be a serious problem and has the potential to destroy relationships at all levels in one's life. We become angry when we experience, or perceive being:

- Hurt.
- Rejected, real or perceived.
- Disabled with physical, social, financial, intellectual deficits.
- A victim of favoritism in childhood that can produce painful memories and emotions that when triggered can evoke anger.

Hurts from the past need to be healed along with forgiving those who caused them. Life's hurts do not stop even after we have recovered from the past. It is necessary to deal with them throughout our lifespan.

It is important to recognize and seek healing regarding your triggers for anger. The goal is to respond in healthier, more godly ways to hurts. Being disrespected, talked down to or embarrassed by others can trigger anger in me. This is due to having my childhood mistakes being told to others to gain a laugh by one of my parents. Spending time with the Lord has greatly healed me from this but occasionally I respond imperfectly.

> *We use sinful (unrighteous) anger to control, suppress, or manage fear and other negative feelings.*

We use sinful (unrighteous) anger to control, suppress, or manage fear and other negative feelings. The spirit of Jezebel attacks many individuals who have been deeply hurt by others. This spirit will attempt to control others through anger, sarcasm, criticism, or finding fault, etc., lashing out in order to keep themselves from feeling vulnerable and feeling negative emotions. Many individuals who have been abused themselves will perpetuate the abusive, hurtful, or angry behavior if not healed and set free by God.

Anger can also be produced when we do not get what we believe is rightfully ours. Frustration is a precursor many times to anger because of our inability to achieve something wanted.

Patience with God, self, and others is key to reducing angry responses. Following God's Word and considering others as better than oneself, (Philippians 2:3) and being merciful and forgiving will produce Christ's life within. The enemy is eager to help us to formulate an offensive reason the person acted toward us, and we become resentful. Many times, our reasoning will be incorrect. Love believes the best of others until proven wrong. This is really key in close relationships such as in marriage. You will overcome unrighteous anger one daily choice at a time.

Pausing when feeling this type of anger and removing yourself from a conversation or a situation is helpful. Pray, asking God to show you what is being triggered and cast your cares onto the Lord. You can always come back and discuss the issue with the other person when the strong feelings have calmed.

One example: someone is driving too slow in front of you, and you are in a hurry! You can pray, take some deep breaths, and choose to relax and be gracious to the driver.

Anger and fear work closely together, as in the natural fight or flight dynamic God has placed in us. The Spirits of Anger and Fear will exaggerate and corrupt our safety fight or flight response to danger. People will identify feeling fear as something to avoid. Fear is painful and tormenting. Addictions are but one maladaptive behavior people will choose to suppress the painful underlying emotion of fear.

8
HEART LEVEL HEALING AND CHANGE

It is vital that we understand believing with one's heart as stated in Romans 10:10, "For it is with your heart that you believe." If your heart believes that God will reject you or abandon you because of the way your parents treated you, then it is difficult to believe that God is good. These wounds or hurts need to be healed before the false belief can be uprooted and foundational truths of God's Word can replace the false belief.

The tendency of the human heart toward pride and self-focus opposes the truth concerning God's perfect character and His Word. It is these ungodly thinking systems or structures with their ungodly companion behaviors that Jesus Christ came to destroy. Even if one recognizes these lies, mental awareness is not enough. These lies must be rooted out at the heart level as we believe with the heart. This is Jesus-level healing, and it is the anointing that breaks the yoke of bondage of sins rooted in pride and self. Jesus came to set the captives free, free from bondage to sin and free to know and operate in the love of God. It is the knowing of the written Word and the Living Word (Jesus Christ) that will bring

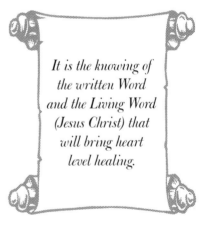

It is the knowing of the written Word and the Living Word (Jesus Christ) that will bring heart level healing.

heart level healing. Every time the human heart embraces knowing and trusting that God is good the heart is softened, leading to repentance from a hard unbelieving heart. "Or do you despise the riches of His goodness, forbearance, and long suffering, not knowing that the goodness of God leads you to repentance," Romans 2:4.

So, if we believe with our hearts as in Romans 10:10 in the first line above, how does our reading of the Word get into the heart? We can practice:

1. **Repenting from believing the false**. This prepares the heart to receive and to be receptive or fertile ground for the seed of the Word to root, grow, and to produce much fruit! "Therefore lay aside all filthiness and overflow of wickedness, and receive the meekness the implanted

Word which is able to save your souls," James 1:21. In 2 Corinthians 3:2, Paul told believers that they were a letter written of Christ, written not with ink but by the Spirit of the living God, not on tablets of stone but on tablets of flesh, that is of the heart.

2. **Get the Word into your heart** - Deuteronomy 6:5-7 "thou shalt love the Lord thy God with all thine heart, and with all thy soul, and with all thy might. And these words which I command you today shall be in your heart:"
   - You shall TEACH them to children, (learning and imparting the truth).
   - You shall TALK of them when you sit in house (confession of your mouth based on God's Word/Spirit during your social and leisure time with yourself and others).
   - When you WALK by the way (be a doer of the word during all activities of life by the power of the Holy Spirit).
   - When you LIE down (know the rest of God available through the Word/Spirit).
   - When you RISE up (start your day off with the Living and Written Word).

3. **Acknowledge the Indwelling of God** as you gaze at the Son through the reading of His Word. We can encounter God every time we read His Word and accept the reality of its contents by doing the following:
   - Read each section of it with the revelation that the Holy Spirit is within you to lead you to encounter the Son .
   - Read it through the power of the Holy Spirit to change you from glory to glory.
   - Read it and choose to accept God's word as truth to you personally.
   - Read it and believe that you are being transformed into that Word.
   - Read it repenting of any sin of unbelief you have identified (lies you believe which are contrary to God's Word).
   - Ask Holy Spirit to reveal any woundedness associated with the lies that needs to be healed.
   - Read the Scriptures, repenting for any sin you identify and asking God's forgiveness and healing.

When we repent, God enables us to turn from our sinful attitudes, behaviors, and ways, and the work Christ did on the Cross becomes fully effective in our lives, and the Lord forgives our sins. We become free from the bondage of our sins and find joy. The purpose of repentance is to restore us to a right relationship with God. God requires obedience but like all spiritual growth this can be a process dependent upon our willingness, our heart, and our behavioral actions toward change. Repentance becomes a joy when one is in love: "If you love me, keep my commandments," John 14:15.

Love not earned but received from God will produce a desire to repent in order to draw closer and closer to the One who first loved you.

The following three chapters will address how to take action against depression, fear, and anger.

9
SPIRITUAL AND BEHAVIORAL ACTIONS AGAINST DEPRESSION

Depression is a mood disorder that causes a persistent feeling of sadness. Some symptoms of depression may include the following:

Feelings:	Thoughts:	Behaviors:	Biochemical:
Anger.	Painful thoughts (introspection i.e. "I am a nobody," or "nothing ever works out for me.")	Acting out or violence. Agitation. Crying. Overeating, or not eating enough.	Constipation, Diarrhea, Difficulty concentrating,
Anxiety.			
Frustration.			
Guilt.	Ruminating over past mistakes.	Sleeping too much or too little. Substance use or abuse (i.e., alcohol, marijuana, etc.). Withdrawing from people and activities.	Insomnia or early morning awakening.
Hopelessness.			
Irritability.	Self-debasing (i.e., "I am no good, I ruin everything.")		Low energy.
Moodiness.	Suicidal or death wish thinking.		Menstrual irregularities.
Sadness.			
Self-anger or Self-hatred, Self-blame.			Tension headaches.
Worthlessness.			

* Note: depression is the leading cause of suicide. Should you have thoughts of wanting to kill yourself or die, contact your medical provider, minister, or national suicide prevention lifeline at 9-8-8, or call 9-1-1 immediately.

Contact your medical provider to rule out any physical cause for the depression. Medication can be helpful in order to correct the biochemical imbalance in the body while you work on choosing God's path and purpose for your life.

SPIRITUAL ACTIONS TO TAKE AGAINST DEPRESSION:

Identify and repent for both personal sins and ancestral sins using the forgiveness prayer ancestors/self/curses for the following sins associated with depression. (Prayers can be found in Appendix A.)

Ancestral Sins, Personal Sins and Demonic Oppression Associated with Depression.
Pray about any of the following that apply to you or your family line.

Anger	Fatigue	Perfectionism
Abandonment	Fear	Poverty
Anxiety	Gluttony	Pride
Broken Heart	Grief	Rejection
Condemnation	Guilt	Self-Pity
Criticalness	Headaches	Self-Rejection/Hatred
Cruelty	Hopelessness	Shame
Crying	Hurt	Sorrow
Death	Indifference	Suicidal thoughts/attempts
Defeatism	Insomnia	Tiredness
Despair	Negative Introspection	Torment linked to unforgiveness or bitterness
Discouragement	Irritability	Whining
False burden	Negativity	Withdrawal
False guilt	Oversleeping	Wounded Spirit
Father/Mother Hurts	Passivity	Poverty

SPIRITUAL ACTIONS TO GAIN/MAINTAIN FREEDOM FROM DEPRESSION

- Knowing God is always good is an essential foundation to believing His Word in all circumstances.
- Seek first the kingdom of God (ask God for His grace to do these things daily). You will be blessed, changed, and healed as you get to know Him. Remember, the enemy doesn't just work 9-5 Monday through Friday. You need to remain alert and stand in the battle for your mind.
- As soon as you wake up you must take control over your thoughts and emotions to align them with God's Word. Declare aloud His Word such as the following:
  1. "Why are thou cast down O my soul? And why art thou disquieted within me? Hope thou in God; for I shall yet praise Him; Who is the health of my countenance and my God?" Ps 42:11.
  2. "The righteous cry, and the Lord heareth, and delivereth them out of all their troubles," Ps 34: 17-18.
  3. "Casting all your care upon Him, for he careth for you," 1 Peter 5:7.
  4. "To give unto them the garment of praise for the spirit of heaviness," Isaiah 61:3.
- Spend time in the presence of God, remembering that He lives within you. Turn your attention to Him through variations of the following:
  1. Worship music.
  2. View His attributes as seen in the Word or in devotionals.
  3. Wait on Him – see Chapter Four: Encountering God.
  4. Acknowledge that the God of the Universe lives within you throughout your day.
  5. Praise Him with scripture.
- Read or listen to God's Word regarding depression and success in life etc. and declare God's Word aloud throughout the day (you can do this so only you can hear it. Do not wait until you feel depressed to declare God's Word. Be proactive. Run into God and His Word by faith and in your spirit. "The name of the Lord is a strong tower: the righteous runneth into it and is safe," Proverbs 18:10.
- Take depressed or downcast feelings and negative thoughts captive unto the Lord by casting them onto Jesus as soon as you are aware of them. An actual transaction takes place when you drop off your depressed feelings and negative thoughts at His feet and walk away from them. You may have to do this frequently in the beginning but you are going from strength to strength in Him and it will become easier. Make a choice to submit to God's Word and resist the enemy. You are dealing with a demon of Depression or Heaviness. Tell it to go in Jesus' name.
- Pray:
  1. With thanksgiving focusing on the good in your life.
  2. To be filled with the Holy Spirit and pray in the Spirit as often as possible.
  3. Request that others pray for you.
  4. Ask the Lord for help daily in time of need before attempting life's activities.
  5. Ask the Lord for His wisdom, favor, and anointing.
  6. Fast and pray as God leads.

7. Praise/worship God.
8. Pray that God leads you not into temptation and delivers you from evil.
9. For protection over your mind and body morning and night, requesting His angels to surround you and your home, office, etc.

BEHAVIORAL ACTIONS TO GAIN/MAINTAIN FREEDOM FROM DEPRESSION:

- Practice the art of gratitude for even minor and major things in your life. I used to work with physically challenged individuals who could not walk, write, read, feed themselves, etc. If you are breathing, reading, able to move on your own, even in a wheelchair, you have reason to be grateful.
- Guard your mouth by speaking God's Word or positive things about self and others.
- Avoid individuals who are critical, negative, or depressed as much as possible.
- Spend time with family and friends and the Body of Christ
- Read books on improving relationships, communication skills, job/career skills, spiritual growth, inspirational individuals who overcame great difficulties, etc.
- Write goals for your life and create a plan to achieve them.
- Note that we depend upon God, but He will not live your life for you. You must not wait for life to come to you. This is called passivity. You can achieve the goals that the Lord has planned for you. God wants you to have friends, family, a career etc. Yes, even failing at times is part of life. Through work and diligence in the power of the Holy Spirit you can succeed. Failure never means that you are a failure.
- Avoid depressing media outlets.
- Exercise routinely i.e., walking, etc. which produces feel good hormones in the body.
- Smile at regular scheduled intervals throughout the day (I love this one it works).
- Eat healthy, avoiding highly processed foods filled with sugar, salt, and fats. Think fruits and vegetables.
- Be kind to yourself and others and celebrate small and big successes.
- Be teachable in order to change negative ways of acting/reacting and bad habit patterns. (Note: changing behaviors takes time, effort, and practice.)
- Write down what you would like to change in your behavior(s) and attitude(s), and create a plan based on God's Word and Holy Spirit's guidance.
- Accomplish something big or small each day.
- Do not let your feelings dictate your life.
- Seek help from ministers, counselors etc. when struggling.

10

SPIRITUAL AND BEHAVIORAL ACTIONS AGAINST ANXIETY, FEAR, AND PANIC ATTACKS

Anxiety is the mind and body's reaction to stress, danger, uncertainty, or unfamiliar situations. Fear is a painful or tormenting feeling initiated by an expectation of evil or an apprehension of impending danger. It can be experienced in degrees, for example, dread, terror, fright. Worry focuses one's mind on difficulty or trouble.

Some of the symptoms of anxiety, fear and *panic attacks include:
(Note: Symptoms with an asterisk are often associated with panic attacks.)

Feelings:	Thoughts:	Behaviors:	Biochemical:
Anger.	Painful thoughts:	Acting out or	*Chest pain.
Depression.	1. Ruminating over past	violence.	*Diarrhea.
Dread.	mistakes	Addictions.	*Difficulty
Distraction.	2. Self-doubting i.e. "I can't	Agitation.	Breathing.
Embarrassment.	change, I've tried," or	Avoidance	*Difficulty thinking or
Frustration.	"I might say or do the	behaviors.	concentrating.
Impatience.	wrong thing."	Compulsive	Insomnia.
Inability to cope.	3. Intrusive thoughts of	behaviors.	*Irritable bowel.
Irritability.	embarrassing or hurtful	Crying.	Muscle pain or tension.
Irrationality.	moments, or words said.	Overeating or not	*Rapid heart
Jitters.	4. All or nothing	eating enough.	Rate.
Loss of self-confidence.	statements, i.e.	Sleeping too little.	*Shaking.
Poor judgment.	"Everything in my life	Substance use or	*Sweating.
Mood swings.	is a mess." "I'll never be	abuse (i.e. alcohol,	Tension
Negativity.	any good."	marijuana, etc.).	Headaches.
Feeling overwhelmed.		Unable to make life	*Trembling.
Restlessness.		decisions.	
Worry.			

SPIRITUAL ACTIONS TO TAKE AGAINST ANXIETY AND FEAR

Anxiety/Fear: Identify and repent for both personal sins and ancestral sins using the forgiveness prayer ancestors/self/curses found in Appendix A with the following sins associated with anxiety and fear.

Ancestral Sins, Personal Sins and Demonic Oppression Associated with Fear/Anxiety
Note: Any of the following that apply to you or your family line.

Abuse	Fantasy	Low self-esteem	Self-hatred
Abandonment	Giving or receiving love	Fear of Man	Self-rejection
Accusation	Fear of God	Marriage	Shame
Anxiety	Heights Phobia	Negativity	Shyness
Authority	Headaches	Nightmares	Skepticism
Condemnation	Heart Attacks	Orphaned	Sophistication
Closed in places	Hypertension	Pain	Sorrow
Confrontation	Hypochondria	Panic	Stress
Confusion	Hysteria	Paranoia	Stuttering
Correction	Idleness	Persecution	Success
Danger	Inadequacy	Phobias	Teeth grinding
Darkness	Indecision	Play-acting	Timidity
Death	Indifference	Poverty	Torment connected to bitterness & unforgiveness
Disapproval	Inferiority complex	Pretension	Unbelief
Depression	Insanity	Procrastination	Unworthiness
Distrust	Insomnia	Python Spirit	Unduly Cautious
Doubt	Intimidation	Reclusive	Water Phobia
Embarrassment	Judgement	Rejection	Women/Men
Escapism	Loneliness	Resentment	Worry
Failure	Losing salvation	Self-focus	

SPIRITUAL ACTIONS TO GAIN/MAINTAIN FREEDOM FROM ANXIETY, WORRY, FEAR:

- Knowing God is always good is an essential foundation to believing His Word in all circumstances.
- Seek first the kingdom of God (ask God for His grace to do these things daily). You will be blessed, changed, and healed as you get to know Him. Remember, the enemy doesn't just work 9-5 Monday through Friday. You need to remain alert and stand in the battle for your mind.
- As soon as you wake up you must take control over your thoughts and emotions to align them with God's Word. Declare aloud His Word such as the following:
- "This is the day the Lord hath made, I WILL REJOICE and be glad in it," Psalm 118:24.
- "For God hath not given me the spirit of fear; but of power, and of love and of a sound mind," 2 Timothy 1:7.
- "Be anxious for nothing, but in everything by prayer and supplication with thanksgiving, let your requests be made known to God and the peace of God, which surpasses all understanding, will guard your hearts and minds through Christ Jesus," Philippians 4:6-7.
- Spend time in the presence of God, remembering that He lives within you. Turn your attention to Him through variations of the following:
  1. Worship/praise music.
  2. View His attributes as seen in the Word or in devotionals.
  3. Wait on Him – see Chapter Four: Encountering God.
  4. Throughout the day turn your attention to Him; acknowledge His love for you.
- Read or listen to God's Word regarding anxiety, worry and fears, success in life etc. and declare His Word aloud throughout the day. You can do this so that only you can hear it. Do not wait until you feel anxious to declare God's Word. Be proactive. Run into God and His Word by faith and in your spirit. 'The name of the LORD is a strong tower: the righteous runneth into it and is safe," Proverbs 18:10.
- Take anxious feelings and negative thoughts captive unto the Lord by casting them onto Him as soon as you are aware of them. An actual transaction takes place when you drop off your anxious feelings and negative thoughts in a bag at His feet and walk away from them. You may have to do this frequently in the beginning but you are going from strength to strength in Him
- Submit to God's Word and resist the enemy. You are dealing with a demon of Fear. Tell it to go in Jesus' name.
- Pray:
  1. With thanksgiving, focusing on the good in your life.
  2. To be filled with the Holy Spirit and pray in the Spirit as often as possible.
  3. Ask the Lord for help daily in time of need before attempting life's activities.
  4. Ask the Lord for His wisdom, favor, and anointing.
  5. Fast and pray as God leads.

6. Praise/worship God.

7. Ask God to lead you not into temptation and to deliver you from evil.

8. Plead the blood of Jesus over your mind and body morning/night, requesting that His angels surround you in your home, workplace, school, etc.

BEHAVIORAL ACTIONS TO GAIN/MAINTAIN FREEDOM FROM ANXIETY, WORRY, FEAR:

- Take any necessary action to reduce the problem causing the worry i.e., to look for a new job or take job skill training or classes, etc.
- Avoid procrastination on home, school, work projects, studying, preparing, etc.
- Read books on improving relationships or communication skills.
- Avoid fear-producing entertainment, i.e. horror or vampire shows and news.
- Avoid individuals who sow fear as God leads.
- Avoid highly processed foods, eliminate caffeinated drinks, high sugar products or food additives.
- Exercise routinely i.e., walking, etc. and when feeling anxious or stressed.
- Perform deep breathing exercises throughout the day. Get comfortable either in a lying or seated position with your shoulders, head and neck supported against the back of the chair. Breathe in through your nose allowing your abdomen to fill with air. Breathe out through your nose. Place one hand on your abdomen and the other on your chest. Feel your abdomen rise when you breathe in and lower when you breath out. The hand on your abdomen should move more than the one on your chest. Take three more full, deep breaths. (Source: Web MD.com.)
- Smile at regular scheduled intervals throughout the day.
- Obtain help from an individual trained in emotional healing and deliverance.
- Listen to Christian worship, meditation, and praise music.
- Attend church services routinely.
- Listen to audio scriptures on faith and fear.
- Stick to a regular sleep schedule. Avoid heavy or large meals a couple of hours before bedtime. Avoid nicotine, caffeine, and alcohol. Keep your bedroom cool, dark, and quiet. Limit daytime naps. Include physical activity in your daily routine. Resolve worries or concerns before bedtime, i.e. jot down what is on your mind and then set it aside for tomorrow. (Source: Mayoclinic.org).
- Take regular breaks from social media.

SPIRITUAL AND BEHAVIORAL ACTIONS FOR PANIC ATTACKS

Panic attacks are acute episodes of fear that trigger physical reactions when there is no real danger or apparent cause. It is important to think prevention. Do not wait until you are having a panic attack to do the following actions. Perform these measures throughout the day at set times. Set your phone or timer to remind yourself. Envision yourself performing these actions as you declare them.

PANIC/ANXIETY ATTACK PRAYERS AND DECLARATIONS:

a. **Move to safety** - Proverbs 18:10 The Lord is a strong tower; the righteous runneth into it and is safe (envision yourself running into the Lord).

b. **Begin your deep breathing exercises** (control them and focus on them).

Note: Only do four cycles of the following at a time to prevent lightheadedness:

1. Close your lips and inhale through your nose for a count of four.
2. Hold your breath for a count of four.
3. Exhale completely through your mouth for a count of four.
4. This completes one cycle.

c. **Envision your statements when declaring them** (example: as seeing yourself casting or dropping your fear/anxiety off onto the Lord or at His feet).

d. **Declare the following:**
1. I cast all my fear/anxiety onto the Lord for He cares for me.
2. I have the breath of life in Jesus.
3. I shall not die but live and declare the works of the Lord.
4. I have all the peace I need as I keep my mind stayed on the Lord.
5. I feel myself relaxing.
6. I feel happy as I trust the Lord (force a smile).
7. My heart is beating with the rhythm of life in Jesus.
8. I am not alone: God is here with me, helping me, strengthening me, and loving me.
9. My life is in control because I belong to the one who controls it all.

e. **Repeat all steps as needed** or one or a few that you find helpful.

11
SPIRITUAL AND BEHAVIORAL ACTIONS AGAINST ANGER

Anger is an emotion precipitated by a real or supposed injury, usually accompanied by a propensity to take vengeance. This emotion can vary in degrees of intensity i.e., mildly disturbed, to rage and violence. Note: frustration is often a precursor to anger. Anger can be expressed inwardly toward self, outwardly toward others, or passively in indirect ways such as giving someone the silent treatment.

Feeling the emotion of anger is not a sin, especially when it is righteous as explained in Chapter 7. It is a sin when the motive behind it is selfish, not glorifying God, becomes chronic, harms others, is vengeful or unforgiving and produces other negative emotions such as depression or irritability.

The following may be signs or symptoms of anger:

Feelings:	Thoughts:	Behaviors:	Biochemical:
Blame.	Painful thoughts:	Acting out or violence.	Difficulty Breathing.
Feelings of wanting to hurt someone or oneself.	1. Ruminating over past hurts from others.	Agitation. Clenching fist.	Difficulty thinking or
Frustration.	2. Negative self-talk, i.e. "I'm so stupid."	Pounding on wall or desk.	concentrating.
Guilt.	3. "There is no justice anymore."	Raising one's voice.	Elevated B/P.
Impatience.	4. "They are idiots."	Substance use or abuse (i.e., alcohol,	Headache.
Irritation when unable to control people or events.	5. "I'm not going to stay at this job."	marijuana).	Muscle pain or tension.
Irritability.	6. "I am going to tell her how rude she is."	Yelling. Passive- aggressive:	Rapid heart Rate.
Irrationality.	7. "This church will never get any better."	1. Indirect refusal.	Shaking.
Isolating from others.		2. Ghosting.	Stomach upset.
Numbness.		3. Lateness.	Sweating.
Resentment.		4. Silence or not responding.	
Sadness.			

Slighted. Superior. Taking offense.		5. Excuses. 6. Acting superior. 7. Sarcasm. 8. Negative body language.	

Anger: Identify and repent for both personal sins and ancestral sins using the forgiveness prayer ancestors/self/curses prayer found in Appendix A, with the following sins associated with anger.

Ancestral Sins, Personal Sins and Demonic Oppression Associated with Anger.
Note: Any that apply to you or your family line.

Addictions	Fighting	Resentment
Anger	Hatred	Retaliation
Apathy	Irritability	Revenge
Argumentativeness	Jealousy	Sabotage
Attention-Deficit/ Hyperactivity Disorder	Meanness	Sarcasm
Bipolar Disorder	Murder	Self-harm (cutting, head banging, burning)
Bitterness	Neglect	Self-rejection
Blame	Obsessions/Compulsions	Self-hatred
Crabbiness	Offended Easily	Silent treatment
Control	Opposition	Stubborn
Criticalness	Passive-aggressive	Sulking
Cruelty	Pride	Temper tantrum
Depression	Rage	Uncooperativeness
Disappointment	Rejection	Violence

SPIRITUAL ACTIONS TO GAIN/MAINTAIN FREEDOM FROM UNRIGHTEOUS ANGER:

- Knowing God is always good is an essential foundation to believing His Word in all circumstances.
- Seek first the kingdom of God. Ask God for grace to do all these things daily. You will be blessed, changed, and healed as you get to know Him. Remember, the enemy does not just work 9-5 Monday through Friday. You need to remain alert and stand in the battle for your mind. As soon as you wake up, you must take control over your thoughts and emotions to align them with God's Word. Declare aloud His Word such as the following:
  1. "Refrain from anger and forsake wrath! Fret not yourself; it tends only to evil," Psalm 37:8.
  2. "A soft answer turns away wrath, but a harsh word stirs up anger," Proverbs 15:1.
  3. "Let all bitterness and wrath and anger and clamor and slander be put away from you along with all malice," Ephesians 4:31.
- Spend time in the presence of God, remembering that He lives within you. Turn your attention to Him through variations of the following:
  1. Worship music.
  2. His attributes as seen in the Word or in devotionals.
  3. Wait on Him – see Chapter 4: Encountering God.
  4. Throughout the day turn your attention to Him, recognizing that the God of the Universe lives within you and loves you.
- Read or listen to God's Word regarding anger, hatred, murder, rejection, fear, etc. and declare His Word aloud throughout the day. You can do this so that only you can hear it. Do not wait until you feel angry to declare God's Word. Be proactive.
- Run into God and His word by faith and in your spirit. "The name of the LORD is a strong tower: the righteous runneth into it and is safe," Proverbs 18:10.
- Take anger, frustration, and negative thoughts captive unto the Lord by casting them onto Him as soon as you are aware of them. An actual transaction takes place when you drop off your angry feelings and negative thoughts in a bag at His feet and walk away from them. You may have to do this frequently in the beginning, but you are growing from strength to strength in Him.
- Submit to God's Word and resist the enemy. You are dealing with a demon of Anger/Rejection/Fear, etc. Tell it to go and leave you in Jesus' name.
- Do not submit to ungodly spirits operating in others. If someone is rejecting you, etc., continue to operate in the fruits of the Spirit which are love, joy, peace, patience kindness, gentleness, and self-control.
- Note: It is Godly to hate evil so go ahead and deal violently with a demonic entity, but not the person the demon is using to attack you.
- It is so important to remember that "we wrestle not against flesh and blood but against powers, against the rulers of the darkness of this world, against spiritual wickedness in high places," Ephesians 6:12.

BEHAVIORAL ACTIONS TO GAIN/MAINTAIN FREEDOM FROM UNRIGHTEOUS ANGER :

- Identify things in your life that can make you angry.
- Pray and ask God what hurt is being triggered or seek a counselor or minister for help regarding anger triggers. Seek healing prayer as needed.
- Identify scripture verses to address areas that need to be healed and transformed by the renewing of your mind.
- Develop a plan based on your anger triggers which include the following:
  1. Confess and choose to repent of unrighteous and chronic unhealthy angry responses to people and life events.
  2. Confess God's Word regarding your new way of thinking and responding to potential hurts, offenses, unmet expectations by others. Realize that rarely does anyone gain a positive outcome or benefit from unrighteous anger. In other words, you are just hurting yourself and your relationships through your anger.
  3. Choose to react in kindness and forgiveness before situations or others trigger your anger. Consider writing down ahead of time how you would respond to an offense by another.
  4. Choose to be patient with others and to thoroughly listen to them before speaking on a matter.
  5. When first aware of angry feelings ask God for help, deep breath, and smile!!!!! Yes, I said smile. It is hard to stay angry when you are smiling.
  6. Set up a separate time when you are no longer feeling angry to discuss issues with a loved one or co-worker. Create a written plan of time in order to keep the discussion from diverting off the real issues at hand.
- Remember, blessed are the merciful for they shall receive mercy.
- Read books on improving relationships or communication skills.
- Avoid anger-producing entertainment, news, people (bind demon of anger and contention in areas or people where you have authority).
- Avoid highly processed foods and eliminate caffeinated drinks, high sugar products or food additives such as MSG.
- Exercise routinely such as walking, and when feeling anxious or stressed.
- Ensure getting enough rest and sleep.
- Perform deep breathing exercises throughout the day.
- Smile at regular scheduled intervals throughout the day (I love this tip - it works).
- Obtain help from an individual trained in emotional healing and deliverance.
- Listen to worship or Christian meditation music, etc.

12
MINISTRY STEPS TO FREEDOM
FOR SELF AND OTHERS

These steps are written for use in ministry settings leading individuals (even groups) into freedom. The steps can be applied by an individual leading oneself through the healing work as well. (See Appendix A for prayers.).

Receive assistance from one experienced or trained to facilitate emotional healing and deliverance as needed. It is best to remove legal rights of demons through the repenting and healing steps before performing deliverance. Lead the individual receiving ministry through the prayers at the end of this chapter. It is important to allow the Holy Spirit to lead and guide. Should a ministry team be used, only one person should lead at a time to avoid creating an atmosphere of confusion or even competition. This can be a very fluid repetitive process. Ensure the individual being ministered to is physically comfortable and has been informed of the steps of this process. It is best to document this informed consent with their signature. Should you or the individual being

It is best to remove legal rights of demons through the repenting and healing steps before performing deliverance.

ministered to want to stop at any point during the ministry session, it is important that this request be honored. Monitor the individual's reactions throughout the session. Should demonic entities manifest bind them by name or by their action. Ensure all legal rights have been removed should demons refuse to leave. Schedule a new session when indicated based on the individual's response and their physical or spiritual needs.

Note: All symptoms are not rooted in emotional problems or demons. Ensure that you or the ministry receiver has been evaluated by a healthcare provider to rule out such things as atrial fibrillation, hyper or hypothyroidism, high blood pressure, iron or vitamin deficiencies, Attention-Deficit/ Hyperactivity Disorder, Bipolar Disorder, allergies to foods, food colorings, hypoglycemia, etc. Physical conditions can greatly impact our mood and our ability to control our words and behaviors.

1. The person receiving ministry must have received salvation through Jesus Christ. before starting, you can ask the person receiving ministry to use the prayer to receive Jesus Christ as Savior and Lord at the end of Chapter 2.

2. The individual needs to be serious about getting set free.

3. Pray before starting, allowing the Holy Spirit to lead, remembering the Holy Spirit resides within you. Rest in His ability to bring the healing desired. It is His love that will heal.

4. Take authority over and bind any demon that would block or interrupt your time with the Lord (see Deliverance Prayer(s) in the Appendix).

5. Ask the person receiving ministry to confess, repent, and ask for God's forgiveness for each judgment made toward parents or those who raised the person. Have them do this by listing all undesirable characteristics of their parents or those who raised them, along with the parents' failure(s) to meet their needs emotionally, physically, or socially. Ask them to forgive parent(s) for each item identified.

6. Have the individual acknowledge and state repentance for sins of their ancestors and self, i.e., depression, self-pity, anxiety, anger, and other sins associated with this stronghold, (see lists in Chapter 9,10 or 11). Have the person receiving ministry ask God for His forgiveness of these sins.

7. Have the individual then forgive their parents and others as the Holy Spirit leads.

8. Allow Holy Spirit to identify core lies that they have believed about God, self, others that do not agree with God's Word and character. Have the person confess, repent, and renounce the lies. Replace the lies with God's Word.

9. Invite the Holy Spirit to reveal:
   a. ungodly vows or oaths.
   b. judgments of others.
   c. bitter-root expectations.
   d. negative attitudes to normal life activities such as school, work, etc.
   e. self-curses/curses by others.
   f. ungodly soul ties.
   g. benefits to having the problem

10. Have the person confess, repent, ask for God's forgiveness, and renounce vows, oaths, judgments, bitter-root expectations, and negative attitudes to normal life activities, benefits to having the problem as God reveals. Repeat all previous actions but add breaking self-curses and ungodly soul ties.

11. Have the person receiving ministry invite Holy Spirit to reveal memories, hurts, wounds, trauma etc. occurring through time periods as follows: in the womb, infancy,1-5 yrs old, 6-10yrs old, 10-20 yrs old etc. Have the individual give the Lord permission to bring healing to the wound. He/she may mentally experience the memory again. In order to provide emotional distance from the traumatic experience, suggest they watch it happen as if on a

screen in their mind. Take note of the predominant negative emotion(s) that accompany the event. Have the person receiving ministry identify the negative emotion(s) and hand each one to the Lord. They may encounter the Lord as Father, Son, or Holy Spirit. God may place a thought into the person's spirit or allow them to experience His love. He knows exactly what each individual needs for healing. Be aware that hurts and trauma may be experienced while a person is still in their mother's womb and during infancy. God is able to reveal and heal these wounds.

12. Ask the person to forgive all who have hurt them through their identified actions/inactions.

13. Bind and cast out the spirit from soul, spirit, and body for each problem, starting with the strongman identified, then followed by the lesser spirits as the Holy Spirit leads. Command all demons to be bound and to separate from each other before casting them out. You do not need to yell as demons are not deaf but you should use a commanding voice when commanding them to "Go in the Name of Jesus." Assure the individual being ministered to that you are not talking to them but to the demon who has been oppressing them. Note: demons may leave once their legal rights have been exposed and repented of without having to cast them out.

14. Wait on the Lord as directed to receive His forgiveness and His refreshing as promised.

15. Finally, pray for all areas vacated by demons to be filled with the Holy Spirit.

16. Loose the opposite Godly fruit into the individual's life to replace each ungodly behavior(s) or attitude(s). See examples below:

Sin or Ungodly Behavior	Opposite Replacement Fruit
Sexual	Purity, self-control
Idolatry (coveting someone/something before God)	God as First Love
Sorcery or occultism	Trust in God
Strife, jealousy, anger, selfishness, discord	Love, peace, patience, kindness, goodness, gentleness, self-control
Anxiety, worry, self-pity	Trust in God, faith

13

ABIDING IN CHRIST AND THE ARMOR OF GOD

Abiding in Christ starts with acknowledgment of the presence of the Holy Spirit who dwells within the believer, "your body is the temple of the Holy Spirit, which is in you," 1 Corinthian 6:19 . Your revelation of the nearness and continual access to the Spirit of God will increase your desire for righteousness, holiness, and intimacy with Him. It will grow the belief that the God who chose to live within His child unconditionally loves His child. This abiding relationship is done by faith in the unseen reality of His word through the power of the Holy Spirt. Note: The unseen is the real and the material is the merely apparent. God gives visible objects their reality. Habitually thinking about Him as with any loved one along with submission of your will to His commandments is required for an abiding relationship in Christ as told in Chapter 4.

God tells us to fight the good fight of faith in 1 Timothy 6:12. We are in a daily battle to overcome the enemy's attacks against us individually, corporately, and even regionally, nationally, and internationally for those called. We are also in a daily battle to overcome our flesh. Spiritual Warfare begins with the knowledge of Christ as the Lord of Hosts which signifies, He has pre-eminence in the universe over all that is good, evil and in between.

Abiding in Christ is based on an intimate relationship with Him. Relationship with another constitutes loving thoughts, feelings, communication, actions etc. It requires being devoted to learning and understanding the heart and mind of the other so as to become joined in thought and purpose. Only Christianity is based on relationship with a Holy God through a Holy Redeemer (Jesus Christ) who indwells the believer with His Holy Spirit.

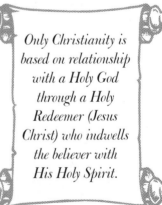

Only Christianity is based on relationship with a Holy God through a Holy Redeemer (Jesus Christ) who indwells the believer with His Holy Spirit.

A.W. Tozer wrote in his book, <u>Pursuit of God</u> that Christians can become so enamored by God's word that they forget God is a person. He has feelings, likes, and dislikes, desires, etc. We are made in His image and given His Holy Spirit when we are born again in order to be in a relationship with Him. "What does relationship have to do with the armor of God?" you might be thinking. Everything in God's kingdom is based on relationship. Relationship is based on communicating love in both word and deed.

Love is not primarily affectionate feelings but also encompasses righteousness and justice. Here is an example: if I love someone, I will not allow them to touch a hot stove without moving them out of the way and possibly scolding them so as not to repeat the dangerous action. God's love for His creation includes adverse outcomes for ignoring His spiritual and natural laws.

Jesus fought the enemy with the rhema word in Luke 4:1 when He quoted, "man does not live by bread alone but by every word that proceeds from the mouth of God," Deuteronomy 8:3. A rhema word is a specific word for the occasion based on inspiration of the Holy Spirit. Jesus modeled for us how to fight the enemy. Remember Jesus only did what He saw His Father doing because He was in close relationship with His Father. The Holy Spirit or the Spirit of Christ "leads us into truth," John 16:12-13. Jesus is the way, the truth, and the life, John 14:6. God's word is truth. Knowing truth is knowing Christ. John 1:1 says, "In the beginning was the word and the word became flesh." This verse recognizes that the word is a person and is distinct in the Godhead. Remember when you are praying, that is, talking to God who is a person allow Him to answer back. This means that when conversing with Him we can honor Him by waiting on Him to speak back to you as you would in any relationship with another. We can expect Him to answer us back. For example when you ask to be filled with His Spirit, wait on Him to fill you. Note: God's word is a primary tool the Holy Spirit will use to speak to you. The more word stored in your heart, the more words, thoughts, and ideas Holy Spirit will have to speak through.

Let us rethink how we put on the armor of God in terms of our relationship with the One Who knows all things. God knows every move of the enemy before it occurs. He knows all of our strengths and weaknesses. He is our Helper in all things. We are to "put on the whole armor of God, that ye may be able to stand against the wiles of the devil," Ephesians 6:11. Each armor piece can represent changing strategies given to us from the Lord.

God knows every move of the enemy before it occurs.

Using the armor of God, here are examples of how to relate to God as you fight this good fight of faith. Our faith is in Him and the truthfulness of His Word.

1. **Belt of Truth** - Put on the Belt of Truth and declare: "I am accepted in the Beloved," The Belt of Truth is God's Word in the Person of Christ. His Word upholds all that we are to think, say and do. All things are measured and created by His Word and empowered by His Spirit. Ask God to show you today where you are measuring yourself by any other standard, for example, comparing yourself to others or the world's standards.

    It is not easy to swim upstream in a world that is flowing in the river of the lust of the flesh, the lust of the eyes, and the pride of life. Experiential knowledge of the breadth, length, depth, and height of the love of God will fill you with the fullness of the Godhead. Being filled with the Spirit of God and the encountering of His love will enable you to overcome the sinful nature of the world around you. Are you comparing yourself spiritually, financially, socially, physically, intellectually, competently, etc. with others? Comparing yourself to others is a dead end. So how do you overcome when facing this? Growing in the experiential knowledge of God's love enables you to be secure in who He created you to be. Your focus on Him helps you keep your focus off of self. You can push through and ignore the world's treatment of you based on the world's standards and break free from being manipulated by the world's lies and distortions. You can choose to hand others' painful treatment of you over to the Lord because He overcame rejection for you, so that the choice to operate in His life and His love is possible.

2. **Breastplate of Righteousness** - Put on the breastplate and declare: "I am the righteousness of God in Christ Jesus," 2 Corinthians 5:21. A breastplate is a piece of armor covering the chest and the heart. A wound to the chest area can be fatal and the enemy knows that. This is why it is important to ensure your heart is in agreement with God. We are righteous in Christ but experientially we can fall short and need to give daily accounts for our attitudes, thoughts, and actions to the only One who can judge righteously. Our own hearts will deceive us as God's word says. You can ask the Lord to show you any wrong attitude, thought, or action. God said anything that is not of faith is sin, Romans 14:23. That is a tall order from God. What Christ did on the cross makes it possible to daily repent of all unbelief in God's perfect character and His word. My question to God was "Lord, I have believed for decades and still don't see your Word coming to pass. How do I keep believing?" I was impressed with this response from God: Because of the indwelling of the Holy Spirit and His power we can continue to believe one day at a time. Pray, "Lord create in me a clean heart Oh God and renew a right spirit within me," Psalm 51:10.

   Remember that the enemy knows each of us well by our words and actions so let us not give him a breach in our armor by holding onto unconfessed sin. Ask God to show you anyone who has hurt you or your believing you did not measure up at home, school, or work. So as not to get into a cycle of unbelief and failure talk about any shortcomings with the Lord and allow Him to wash you and refresh you before a new day. Yesterday's sins and failures have all been addressed by Christ on the Cross and He has given you His robe of righteousness. As the Holy Spirit once said to me when I was beating myself up for a sin and failure, He said, "Cheryl what made you think there was nothing wrong with you?" I knew that He was pointing out my sin of pride in thinking that I myself am the perfect one, and not the Holy One who resides in me. He is our Redeemer and will redeem all of our failures should we allow Him and can turn them into good for us and His glory.

3. **Shoes of the Gospel of Peace**- Put on the Shoes of the Gospel of Peace and Declare: "the kingdom of God is within me and is righteousness, peace and joy in the Holy Spirit." Peace is not just the absence of turmoil or conflict. It is the presence of the King of Kings and the Lord of Lords. We as believers have the honor and privilege of carrying the presence of Christ wherever we go. Our light always overcomes darkness if allowed to shine.

The enemy comes to kill, steal, and destroy but we are to carry life abundantly to those who are hungering and thirsty to hear the good news of the gospel. Declare God's peace and presence wherever you go dispelling darkness and the enemy's stronghold. Our footing is based on the word of God and His character. Ask God to show you if your foundation for each area of your life has moved off of the Word . Ask God to reset your foundation on the Rock which is Jesus Christ. When our hearts are overwhelmed by life's difficulties, we can allow the Spirit to lead us to the Rock who is higher than our thoughts, feelings, troubles, conflicts etc. Allow Him to restore peace whenever needed. "He is our refuge and strength, a very present help in trouble," Psalm 46:1-2. "When done all you can do, stand." Ephesians 6:13. If a soldier can keep his footing, he will be victorious.

4. **Shield of Faith** - Acknowledge you have the shield of faith and declare: "I walk by faith not by sight," 2Corinthians 5:7. It is difficult but not impossible to believe God's Word and the absolute goodness of God's character if one's heart is believing lies as was discussed in Chapter 1. It is impossible to please God without faith and this is why the enemy will do anything to damage it. Paul inspired by the Holy Spirit uses the metaphor of a shield because in his day the shield made the army. Without his shield a Roman soldier was a walking target. A shield was the only real defense. As a unit the Romans could at an order lock their large oval shields together, to create a defensible barrier from which they could launch spear attacks and repel an enemy attack. Behind this moveable barricade they could advance toward a hostile city wall without suffering casualties. The Word of God empowered by the Holy Spirit is our only defense individually as well as corporately. Our shield of faith is in His blood and His name. Plead the blood over your life and declare the name of Jesus to shield you when the enemy comes against you spiritually, physically, emotionally etc. Taking the elements in communion is God's way of resetting our faith on the finished work of the cross. Communion reminds the believer to forgive all who have harmed them. Many times it is those in the Body of Christ who hurt each other. It is imperative that we forgive each other just as Christ has forgiven us so that we are free to lock our faith(shields) with each other in unity. This doesn't mean you have to fellowship with chronic offenders, but forgiveness keeps one's heart free to love and to connect and lock our shields (faith) with those in the body of Christ. God is not only interested in our relationship with Him but our relationship with others.

5. **Helmet of Salvation** - Put on the helmet and declare: "I have the mind of Christ; I will not agree with the accuser of the brethren today." Having the mind of Christ is about humility and saying yes to God's will. Remember, "God resisteth the proud, but giveth grace to the humble," James 4:6. Ask the Father which Scripture verses you need today to overcome the thoughts or fiery darts from the enemy. Wait to hear from the Lord. This is not a formula for conversation with God so be patient as you develop your relationship with God. Set your mind to think on things above today. Remember God speaks to us in many ways i.e. His word, His creation, His Spirit, etc. If you do not think that you have heard from God, choose a bible verse trusting that He prompted you to decide on the one you need for today. Rehearse that verse in your mind and aloud if needed throughout the day. Overcome your

emotions today by declaring, "This is the day the Lord has made, I will rejoice and be glad in it." Realize that you are making a mindful decision to rejoice and you are choosing to be glad. You have control over your thoughts and your thoughts will impact your feelings. Ask God to enable you to "cast down imaginations and every high thing that exalteth itself against the knowledge of God and bringing into captivity every thought to the obedience of Christ," 2 Corinthians 10:5. Turn your focus to the Holy Spirit who lives within you and hand Him the intrusive lies from the enemy. He is real and is within you to empower you to succeed today. Did you recognize that the Helmet of Salvation covers your mind, your thoughts, and your choices?

6. **Sword of the Spirit** – Acknowledge you have the sword of the Spirit and declare: "I am more than a conqueror in Christ Jesus." Charles Spurgeon preached in 1891 that the sword of the Spirit warns of danger, prepares one for warfare and prophesies of opposition. The Spirit of God espouses the cause of love against hate, truth against error, holiness against sin and Christ against Satan.

To conquer means to take control of a people or place by military force or to successfully overcome a problem or weakness. (Source:handspeak.com). I was less than a conqueror until encountering the Living Word in 1994. Something was missing from my relationship with the Lord as told in chapter 4. My heart was delivered from the sin of unbelief regarding the goodness of God during that Toronto meeting. Allowing the Lord to cut through unbelief in all areas of your life will change the seeds of sin and doubt into seeds of righteousness and faith. We are told to submit to God first then to "resist the enemy and He will flee, James 4:7. Submitting to God as revealed in His Word is a precursor to being more than a conqueror.

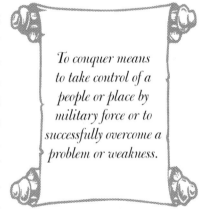

To conquer means to take control of a people or place by military force or to successfully overcome a problem or weakness.

Being in Christ Jesus denotes relationship. This relationship is based on knowing the written and living word intimately. It is based on submitting to the written and living word then wielding the Word like a sword under the power of the Holy Spirit.

It's time to draw a line and take back all that is rightfully yours as identified in both the written and living Word from the enemy. Use the sword of the Spirit to conquer and to plunder the enemy's camp. Those who conquer do not compromise nor do they appease the enemy. Those who fight know the battle is real and do not give up after one or two fights. They continue until the battle is won.

The word of God must be wielded by the Holy Spirit who lives within us and has chosen the word to use for warlike purposes. The word of God empowered through relationship with the Spirit of God will cut deeper than anything in the natural. God's word is a conquering weapon. Jesus used the rhema word which caused the enemy to flee.

14
BIRTHING OR ABORTING PRAYERS

God gives many wonderful promises in His Word regarding prayer. It is important to look at the promises together when discussing the topic. God's Word tells us to ask, and:

1. keep asking,
2. believe that you have received,
3. agree together in prayer,
4. pray God's will,
5. pray continually,
6. be grateful in prayer,
7. do not be doubleminded in prayer,
8. do not ask with wrong motives,
9. abide in Christ and His Word.

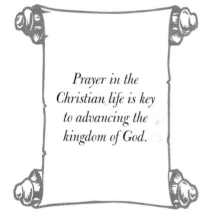

Prayer in the Christian life is key to advancing the kingdom of God.

Prayer in the Christian life is key to advancing the kingdom of God. When we are younger in the Lord, self is still very much on the throne of our lives. Our prayers will be mostly about our own needs. This is not necessarily wrong because God says you have not because you ask not, but His goal is to transform you into the image of His Son. Should you believe God is a vending machine to get you what you want in life, you may find yourself very frustrated.

Your willingness to seek God first for His purposes and trusting God to meet all your needs is essential to victory in prayer. God answers prayers according to His will and His timing. Answered prayer brings glory to Himself and blesses His children. Seek God first through His Word and possibly through fasting before praying to discover what His will is. Once you know what His will is, you can pray with faith.

BIRTHING PRAYER

The story of Hannah in 1 Samuel is a great example of birthing prayer. Hannah was unable to conceive. She sought God year after year in the temple to give her a son. A key to birthing prayer is perseverance. Hannah poured out her heart to the only One who could change her barrenness. God's will was to birth a prophet at the right moment in history through Hannah. But first, her heart required God's transformational work which was accomplished during the course of seeking Him in prayer.

Hannah's waiting for God to answer changed her. Waiting on God changes us. It takes us from glory to glory. God wants to put our hearts at rest in prayer so that we seek the greater, which is to know Him. Hannah was the first person to call God the Lord of Hosts. She grew to know Him and have faith in His sovereign voice that commands all the hosts of heaven and earth. Every atom, every subatomic particle moves according to His purposes and is upheld by His Word. A woman desperate to bear a son to relieve her own barrenness and shame vowed to give God the child if He would command it to be so. Hannah was so transformed through years of prayer that she came to completely trust and choose God's will for her son. Eli, the priest in the temple, spoke a blessing to Hanna. She believed Eli's word for God to answer her prayer request because she had come to know her God through prayer.

God wants to put our hearts at rest in prayer so that we seek the greater which is to know Him.

Let us review some of the points on birthing prayers:

- Seek God first for His will through His Word and His Spirit.
- Seek first the kingdom of God and His righteousness.
- Pray or declare God's Word or prophecy once you know what His will is.
- Persevere in prayer knowing that you have received what you have asked for.
- Continually thank and praise Him for answering prayer and for all that He has done for you.
- Enter the Lord's rest and His provision, and His faithfulness to answer prayers according to His ways and timing.
- Seek to know the Lord of Hosts, God almighty.
- Come into agreement with other believers.
- Obey any instructions God gives through his Word or Spirit concerning your prayer.

ABORTING PRAYER

In the book of Luke, we read the story of Zechariah, John the Baptist's father. He received a visitation of the angel Gabriel while performing priestly duties in the temple. Gabriel announced to him that his prayer for a son had been answered. Zechariah doubted this message because he and his wife were past child-bearing age. After Zechariah asked for proof of the truth of this announcement, he was rendered mute until the birth of John the Baptist. It is important to note that the angel's action to pronounce muteness on Zechariah was necessary for the fulfillment of their prayer and God's will. "Life and death are in the power of the tongue," Proverbs 18:21. God prevented Zechariah from speaking doubt or unbelief for the next 9 months to prevent Satan from having the legal right to abort the baby. How many of our prayers are aborted because of our mouths?

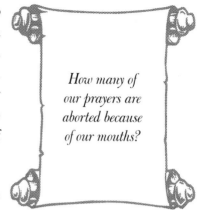

How many of our prayers are aborted because of our mouths?

I asked God why I was seeing so few answers to my prayers. This was His response to my question: "Cheryl, you do not ask in faith. You ask, then you wait and see if it happens. When you do not see anything happen, you get discouraged and quit. If you really believed I was going to answer your prayers, you would not walk away and speak as though the problem or lack still existed. You have aborted your prayers by your mouth."

Here is an example of this: It is God's will for your son or daughter to be saved. You pray for their salvation but continue to talk about them as though they are not changing or going to be saved. You are agreeing with Satan's plan for their life by speaking ill of them. We walk by faith and not by sight. Repent and change your declarations to agree with God's will that they are changing and will come to know Jesus as their Lord and Savior.

<u>Let us review the actions that will abort our prayer</u>:

- Walk by what we see.
- Do not believe God's Word.
- Do not trust God.
- Do not ask in faith.
- Do not ask according to God's will.
- Talk about the problem or lack, instead of declaring or decreeing what we have asked for and thanking Him for the answer.
- Get discouraged and fail to continue to pray.

Prayer for me has been one of the greatest joys in my life as well as one of the most disappointing and discouraging endeavors. I can honestly say that it took me a long time to learn some of these quite simple lessons. God has been exceedingly kind and faithful to me all along my sometimes very bumpy road. I pray that you will use some of these lessons to avoid pitfalls in prayer.

15
DAILY RESET IN GOD

Psalms 1:3 says, "and whatsoever he doeth shall prosper." The word prosper in the Hebrew literally means "to push forward; to pass through; to get on." It carries the idea of succeeding in what you do according to the Strong's Concordance.

1 Chronicles 4:9-10 we find a man named Jabez whose name means sorrow. He moved forward through the pain in his life to be blessed by God. God admonishes His people to move or push forward in life as seen in these verses:

1. Isaiah 43:18 – "Remember ye not the former things, neither consider the things of old."
2. Exodus 14:15-16 - "Speak unto the children of Israel that they go forward."
3. 2 Corinthians 5:17 – "Therefore if any man be in Christ, he is a new creature: old things are passed away, behold all things are become new."
4. John 5:8 – "Jesus saith unto him, Rise, take up thy bed and walk."
5. Proverbs 4:25 – "Let thine eye look right on and let thine eyelids look straight before thee."
6. Luke 9:62 - "And Jesus aid unto him, No man, having put his hand to the plough and looking back is fit for the kingdom of God."

This moving forward and not looking back is critical. Compare chronically looking back to layers of dirt building up on an air filter which impedes the proper functioning of the product. Yesterday's failures, wrong choices, negative experiences, sins, hurts, etc. can hinder moving forward with God's blessings for today. Renewing the mind and resetting the heart daily is analogous to shutting the door on past pain and sorrow. The enemy loves to get us to flounder in yesterday's difficulties. Recognize that all of our mistakes or sinful choices when confessed and repented of give us a fresh start or do-over today. His mercies are utterly new each morning, Lamentations 3:22-23. You may even make the same

Yesterday's failures, wrong choices, negative experiences, sins, hurts, etc. can hinder moving forward with God's blessings for today.

mistake multiple times but choose to believe God 's love and mercy are available for you today. God's children have an opportunity to reset and walk afresh with him every twenty-four hours or sooner if necessary.

Isaiah 55:8-9 - God declares that His ways and thoughts are higher than ours. His greater concern for our spiritual prosperity is evident when He said, " we cannot serve God and mammon," Matthew 6:24. This does not mean that prosperity in God's kingdom only encompasses the spiritual but when we seek God's kingdom or His rule and reign in our lives first then He will add our earthly needs, Matthew 6:33. Our hearts and minds are to be reset in Him daily. Here are suggestions on how to do this:

1. Acknowledge the presence of God within you. Acknowledge the magnitude of His power and greatness, faithfulness, strength, love for you, and His desire to bless you.
2. Ask God to show you or identify areas of failings, sins, mistakes, woundedness, disappointments even with God from yesterday. Practice waiting on Him as you acknowledge His Presence. The Holy Spirit usually gives us thoughts, pictures, memories, or His Word when speaking to us.
3. Repent of any sin i.e. action or belief not in agreement with God's Word.
4. Renounce any agreement, justification, or benefit you have had with the problem or sin.
5. Forgive – self and others associated with the problem or repent of being angry or disappointed in God.
6. Cast all failings, mistakes, woundedness onto the Lord at the cross. Wait on Him to heal or to communicate His love to you.
7. Obtain a bible verse to replace and destroy any wrong thinking associated with the sin or failings.
8. Reset your heart to agree with what God's word says today in any area identified: spiritual, emotional, social, financial, personal, etc. This is why it is so important to know and memorize the word of God so that you know God's will. Begin to declare that bible verse (truth) in order to get it into your heart. Continue this step until your heart believes what God says about you or your situation.

Choose today to agree with God's word for victory and prosperity. Do not let the power of the blood and the cross be wasted nor let the enemy lie to you that resetting or changing is too hard. Fight the good fight of faith through the daily resetting of your mind and heart on God's goodness and the truth of His word. You were created to be an overcomer in this life so that you can rule and reign with Him. You have all the power and self-control needed to accomplish this today through His Spirit.

Choose today to believe or agree with God's Word listed or as Holy Spirit leads you:

Matthew	5:14	I am the light of the world.
John	3:36	I have eternal life.
John	7:38	Out of my innermost being flows rivers of living water.

John	10:10	I have abundant life.
John	13: 34	I have love for others.
John	14: 20	I am in Christ, and Christ is in me.
John	15: 9	I am loved by Jesus.
John	16: 27	I am loved by the Father.
John	8: 32	I know the truth and the truth sets me free.
Romans	1: 7	I am beloved of God.
Romans	5: 5	I have the love of God which has been poured out through Jesus' death.
Romans	6: 1-6	I died with Christ and died to sin's rule over my life.
Romans	8: 28	All things are working together for my good.
Romans	8: 30	I have been justified and glorified.
Romans	8: 37	I am more than a conqueror.
1 Cor.	2:16	I have the mind of Christ.
1 Cor.	6:19	I am a temple of God. Holy Spirit dwells in me.
1 Cor.	6: 20	I have been bought with a price. My body and spirit belong to God.
2 Cor.	2: 14	I always triumph in Christ.
2 Cor.	5: 7	I walk by faith, not by sight.
2 Cor.	5: 17	I am a new creation (new person) in Christ.
2 Cor.	5: 20	I am an ambassador for Christ imploring people to be reconciled to God.
2 Cor.	5: 21	I am the righteousness of God in Christ Jesus.
2 Cor.	9: 8	I have grace from God so I can abound in every good work.
Gal.	2: 20	I am crucified with Christ. I no longer live, but Christ lives in me; and the life I live now, I live by faith.
Gal.	5: 22	I have the fruit of the Spirit: love, joy, peace, patience, kindness goodness, faithfulness, gentleness, and self-control.
Eph.	1: 3	I am blessed with every spiritual blessing in heavenly places in Christ.
Eph.	1: 4	I have been chosen before the foundation of the world to be Holy and without blame before Him.
Eph.	1: 6	I am accepted in the beloved (Christ).
Eph.	1: 13	I have been sealed in Him with the promised Holy Spirit.
Eph.	1: 20	I am seated with Christ in the heavenlies.
Eph.	2: 4	I am loved by God.
Eph.	2: 8-9	I have been saved by grace through faith, it is a gift of God.
Eph.	3: 17	I am rooted and grounded in Christ's love.
Eph.	6: 10	I am strong in the Lord and in the power of His might.
Phil.	1: 6	I am confident that He who began a good work in me will complete it.
Phil.	2: 13	God is at work within me both to will and to do His good pleasure.
Phil.	4: 7	I have the peace of God which passes all understanding.
Phil.	4: 13	I can do all things through Christ who strengthens me.

Phil.	4: 19	I have all of my needs met by God according to His riches in glory in Christ Jesus.
Col.	1: 13	I have been delivered from darkness (Satan's rule) and transferred to the kingdom of His dear Son (Jesus Christ).
Col.	1: 27	Christ in me is the hope of glory.
Col.	2: 10	I have been made complete in Christ.
Col.	3: 3	I am hidden with Christ in God.
2Tim.	1: 7	I have not been given a spirit of fear, but of power, love, and sound mind.
Heb.	4: 16	I can come boldly to the throne of grace with confidence to receive mercy and find grace to help in time of need.
Heb.	13: 5	God will never leave me nor forsake me.
Heb.	13:12	I am made holy through Jesus' own blood.
James	1: 5	God generously and without reproach gives to me wisdom if I ask Him.
1 Peter	1:16	Because He is holy, I am holy.
1 Peter	2:24	I am healed by the wounds of Jesus.
1 Peter	1:18	I was not redeemed with perishable things like silver or gold but with the precious blood of Christ, a lamb without blemish or defect.
1 John	1: 9	If I confess my sins, He is faithful and just and will forgive me and purify me from all unrighteousness.
1 John	4: 4	I have spiritual authority.
1 John	5: 18	I am born of God and the evil one (Satan) cannot touch me.
1 John	5: 4	I have overcome the world.
Rev.	21: 7	I am victorious.
Jer.	31: 3	I am loved with an everlasting love.

APPENDIX A. MINISTRY PRAYERS

I. PRAYER TO RECEIVE THE LORD JESUS CHRIST AS SAVIOR AND LORD:

I believe that there is only one true and living God who exists as Father, Son, and Holy Spirit. I believe that Jesus Christ is the Son of the living God and is Himself God. I believe that Jesus Christ is the Messiah, the Word who became flesh and dwelt among us.

I confess that I am a sinner and ask You Lord to forgive me for all my sins. I believe in your gift of salvation which you bought for me through your death, burial, and resurrection. I choose to repent from what you call sin in your word the Bible. I invite you into my heart to be my Savior and Lord as I submit my life and will to you in Jesus' name, Amen.

II. FORGIVENESS PRAYER FOR SINS OF ANCESTORS/SELF/CURSES

As a child of God, I choose to confess and acknowledge the sins of my ancestors. I choose to forgive and release them and to not hold them responsible for each way that their sins have affected me.

I now renounce all of the sins (name each one identified) of my ancestors and release myself from their effects, based on the finished work of Christ on the Cross.

Lord, I am sorry for all of the ways that I have committed these same sins and allowed the curses to affect me. I ask You to forgive me for this and to wash me clean. I choose to receive Your forgiveness.

I affirm that I have been crucified with Jesus Christ and raised to walk in newness of life. On this basis, I announce to Satan and all his forces that Christ took upon Himself the curses and judgments due me. Thus I break every curse that has come upon me because of my ancestors. I also break all curses that have been released onto me by others. I also break all curses that I have spoken or thought about myself. I receive my freedom from every one of these curses.

Because of the above and because I have been delivered from the power of darkness and translated into the kingdom of God's dear Son, I cancel the legal rights of every demon sent to oppress me.

Because I have been raised up with Christ and now sit with Him in heavenly places, where I have a place as a member of God's family, I renounce and cancel each and every way that Satan and his demons may claim ownership of me. I cancel all dedications made by my ancestors of their descendants, including me and my descendants in the name of Jesus. I declare myself to be completely and eternally owned by, and committed to, the Lord Jesus Christ.

All this I do based on the truth revealed in the Word of God and in the Name and with the Authority of my Lord and Savior, Jesus Christ. Amen!

(Prayer for Sins of Ancestors from Restoring the Foundations by Chester and Betsy Kylstra.)

III. REPENTANCE PRAYERS FOR OCCULT PRACTICES AND SINS

Be specific and name each occultic activity/sin individually out loud.

1. Lord, I am choosing this day to repent from the following sin or occult activity:

   _____

2. Lord, I renounce and no longer want this occult activity or sin in my life and cut all ties to it:

   _____

3. Lord forgive me for participating in the following occult activity or sin:

   _____

4. Lord, I forgive _____(anyone who introduced me to the following occult activities or participated in this sin with me if indicated).

5. Lord, I thank you for forgiving me as I place all these sins on the cross based on your word in 1John 1:9 which says, "If we confess our sins, he is faithful and just to forgive us our sins and to cleanse us from all unrighteousness."

6. Lord I now receive your forgiveness for these sins (pause and wait on the Holy Spirit as He cleanses your spirit, soul, and body from these sins).

7. Lord I now receive your refreshing for these sins that I have repented from according to your word which says, Repent ye therefore, and be converted, that your sins may be blotted out, when the times of refreshing shall come from the presence of the Lord, Acts 3:19.

IV. PRAYER FOR RENOUNCING CURSED OBJECTS

Lord, I come to you about cursed objects and any demon infestation in my possessions, home, or workplace. I ask your forgiveness for having any such items in the precious name of Jesus. I understand that this is idolatry. Please forgive me.

Please show me any cursed objects, symbols, or demon infestation and spirits that need to be cast out. I will cast out the evil spirits out of my house in the precious name of Jesus.

I renounce any ties or expected benefits to having these items.

I receive your forgiveness according to your word that, "If we confess our sins, He is faithful and just to forgive us our sins and to cleanse us from all unrighteousness," 1 John1:9. Thank you for delivering me. Amen.

V. MINISTRY PRAYER FOR BELIEVING LIES ABOUT GOD, SELF, AND OTHERS

1. I confess my sin and my ancestor's sin of believing the lie that: _____.
2. I forgive those who contributed to my forming this lie: (be specific).
3. I ask You, Lord, to forgive me for receiving this lie and for living my life based on it, and for any way I have judged others because of it.
4. I receive your forgiveness.
5. On the basis of Your forgiveness, Lord I choose to agree with You and repent of being angry at myself for agreeing with the lie.
6. I place this anger at myself on the Cross of Jesus Christ.
7. I renounce and break my agreement with this lie. I cancel all agreements with demons.
8. I choose to accept, believe, and receive the Truth based on God's Word that _____
9. I choose to act or behave in a way that is unique to my personality but is based on the truth of God's Word.
10. I will allow myself time to change as my mind is being renewed.
11. I will not quit or believe the enemy or my flesh that this is too hard!

VI. MINISTRY PRAYER FOR UNGODLY SOUL TIE

1. Lord, reveal to me any ungodly soul ties _____.

2. I confess that I have had an ungodly connection with _____ (name person).

3. I repent of this ungodly soul tie based on the sins of _____ (e.g., dependence, fear, immorality, worship, control, anger, hatred/bitterness, manipulation).

4. In the name of Jesus Christ, I renounce, break and loose myself from an ungodly soul tie with the following person(s) _____.

5. I repent of the sinful behavior _____ associated with this ungodly soul tie. In the name of Jesus Christ, I declare the enemy's right to oppress me because of this relationship is now broken because of the victory of Jesus Christ at the Cross.

6. I renounce all soul tie spirits and cast you out of my spirit, soul, and body in Jesus' name.

VII. DELIVERANCE PRAYERS FOR DEPRESSION (SPIRIT OF HEAVINESS)

Use the ministry prayers for each symptom that you are experiencing.

In Jesus' Name I bind spirits of fear, blocking, unbelief, rationalism, and pride that would interfere in my healing and deliverance.

Lord, I give you permission to reveal the truth about any root that has caused or contributed to this depression. (Wait on the Lord as the Spirit brings something to your mind. For traumatic events allow yourself to watch them on a screen and acknowledge your feelings. Identify the negative feelings. Cast the negative feeling of depression etc. onto Jesus.

Ask the Lord to heal any emotional wounds associated with the event.

In Jesus' Name I forgive (name), who contributed to this depression.

In Jesus' Name I acknowledge/confess the sin of depression (spirit of heaviness) in my ancestors and myself.

In Jesus' Name I renounce and repent of the sin of depression.

I renounce any ties or benefits gained with a spirit of depression or heaviness.

In Jesus' Name I bind the strongman of Depression (Spirit of Heaviness). Using His divine weapons I demolish the stronghold of Depression (Spirit of Heaviness).

In Jesus' Name I command you, Spirit of Depression (Spirit of Heaviness) to leave my soul, spirit, body, (conscious/subconscious) now and go to dry uninhabitable places.

In Jesus' Name I receive your forgiveness and refreshing. (Pause as you wait on the Lord and you receive His promises of forgiveness and refreshing.)

Father, I ask you in Jesus' Name to release your Spirit of Joy and Peace into my life.

VIII. DELIVERANCE PRAYERS FOR ANXIETY, FEAR AND WORRY

Use the ministry prayers for each symptom you are experiencing.

In Jesus' Name I bind spirits of fear, blocking, unbelief, rationalism, and pride that would interfere in my healing and deliverance.

Lord, I give you permission to reveal the truth about any root that has caused or contributed to anxiety and fear. (Wait on the Lord as the Spirit brings something to your mind). For traumatic events allow yourself to watch them on a screen and acknowledge your feelings. Identify the negative feelings. Cast the negative feeling of anxiety, fear etc. onto Jesus. Ask the Lord to heal any emotional wounds associated with the event.

In Jesus' name I forgive (name) who contributed to this anxiety, fear, and worry.

In Jesus' Name I acknowledge/confess the sin of anxiety, fear, worry (spirit of anxiety, fear, worry) in my ancestors and myself.

In Jesus' Name I renounce and repent of the sin of anxiety, fear, and worry.

I renounce any ties or benefits gained with a spirit of anxiety, fear or worry.

In Jesus' Name I bind the strongman of Fear. Using His divine weapons I demolish the stronghold of Fear.

In Jesus' Name I command the Spirit(s) of anxiety, fear and worry to leave my soul, spirit, body, (conscious/subconscious) now and go to dry uninhabitable places.

In Jesus' Name I receive your forgiveness and refreshing. (Pause as you wait on the Lord and you receive His promises of forgiveness and refreshing.)

Father, I ask you in Jesus' Name to release your Spirit of Joy and Peace into my life.

IX. DELIVERANCE PRAYERS FOR ANGER:

Use the ministry prayers for each symptom you are experiencing.

In Jesus' Name I bind spirits of fear, blocking, unbelief, rationalism, and pride that would interfere in my healing and deliverance.

Lord, I give you permission to reveal the truth about any root used or contributed to this anger. Wait on the Lord as the Spirit brings something to your mind. For traumatic events allow yourself to watch them on a screen and acknowledge your feelings. Identify the negative feelings. Cast the negative feeling of anger etc. onto Jesus. Ask the Lord to heal any emotional wound associated with the event.

In Jesus' Name I forgive (name) who contributed to this anger.

In Jesus' Name I acknowledge/confess the sin of anger in my ancestors and myself.

In Jesus' Name I renounce and repent of the sin of anger.

I renounce any ties or benefits gained with a spirit of anger.

In Jesus' Name I bind the strongman of Anger. Using His divine weapons I demolish the stronghold of Anger.

In Jesus' Name I command the Spirit(s) of anger to leave my soul, spirit, body, (conscious/subconscious) now and go to dry uninhabitable places. In Jesus' Name I receive your forgiveness and refreshing. (Pause as you wait on the Lord to receive His promises of forgiveness and refreshing.)

Father, I ask you in Jesus' Name to release your Spirit of Joy and Peace into my life.

REFERENCES

Baxter, M. K., (1993). A Divine Revelation of Hell. Whitaker House, New Kensington, PA.

Bickle, M., (1993). Passion for Jesus. Charisma House, Lake Mary, FL.

Clark, D., & Dr. J., (2017). Self-Deliverance Made Simple. Destiny Image, Shippensburg, PA.

King James Version of the Bible. (2018). On-Line-Thomas Nelson, Inc.

Kylstra, C., & Kylstra, B. (2001). Restoring the Foundations. Proclaiming His Word, Inc. Santa Rosa Beach, FL

Merriam-Webster. (2019). Merriam-Webster Dictionary. G. K. Hall & Company.

Springfield, MA.

Minirth, M.D., F. & Meer, P. (2013). Happiness is a Choice. Baker Books. Grand Rapids, MI.

Sanford, P., & Sanford, J., (1982). Transformation of the Inner Man. Elijah House, Rathdrum, ID.

Tozer, A.W. (2020). The Crucified Life. Grapevine India Publishers PVT LTD. Delhi/Mumbai.

Tozer, A.W. The Pursuit of God. Aneko Press. anekopress.com

Printed in the United States
by Baker & Taylor Publisher Services